How to

BUILD WORK TEAM HABITS

IMPROVE YOUR CUSTOMER EXPERIENCE, INCREASE EFFICIENCY, AND ENJOY BETTER BUSINESS RESULTS

KYLE HAVILL

TABLE OF CONTENTS

Introduction..4

Chapter 1: The Habit Development Process....................7

Chapter 2: Determine Which Habits Your Team Should

Develop..23

Chapter 3: Provide Team Members with Habit Development

Knowledge..48

Chapter 4: Plan the First Team Habit......................80

Chapter 5: Complete Your First Habit Development

Worksheet..105

Chapter 6: Prepare to Put the Habit Development Plan

into Action..134

CHAPTER 7: THE CRITICAL ROLE OF LEADERSHIP IN HABIT

DEVELOPMENT...**155**

CHAPTER 8: LAUNCH THE HABIT AND MAKE IT A WAY

OF LIFE...**173**

APPENDIX: LIST OF POTENTIAL TEAM AND INDIVIDUAL

REWARDS..**194**

For Susan

and our children, Michael, Michael, and Lauren

INTRODUCTION •···

HABITS ARE AMAZING ASPECTS of everyday life.

If it weren't for habits, we could barely function.   Imagine if every action you took, no matter how small, required deep thought about how you would move every muscle involved.   The very simple action of walking one step involves up to 200 muscles. Imagine if you had to think through each muscle movement—which ones to move, which direction and how far—and then coordinate this with the other 199 muscles involved.

Thanks to habits, we take several thousand steps a day with very little conscious thought. Habits free up our mind to think and focus on planning to be more effective and efficient, doing work, or just enjoying life.

Once adopted and used for an extended period of time, habits create physiological changes to our brains.   They are "hard wired".   Once they become pathways in our brain, we hardly have to give them a second thought, they become automatic and save us a great deal of effort and stress.

Habits are powerful.

When simple but important actions are not established as habits, we are required to spend conscious effort in taking actions that we might otherwise do automatically. Because there is a limit to the amount of conscious bandwidth we have, this costs us in terms of our potential to add value to our lives and those of others.

We will go into a lot more detail about habits in the first few chapters of the book. For now, it is just essential to recognize the fact that habits are important and powerful.

There are many excellent self-improvement books on the market about personal habit development. These books help people develop useful, powerful habits in their daily living. In reading and applying principles from these books, millions of people have improved their lives, enabling them to be more productive, add more value, and feel more fulfilled.

Knowing all of this leads to an interesting question, however. Why limit the power of habits to personal improvement?

What if we applied habit theory to a group of people, like a work team? What if groups of 3, 30, 300 or more, in a coordinated effort, developed important habits that could improve the customer experience and help the company operate more efficiently? How much additional value could they add? As a team, how much more could these individuals accomplish beyond just the sum of their efforts? What kind of an advantage would this give a company over its competition?

Do you see the possibilities? Are you intrigued?

By the time you finish this book, you will know exactly how to take the incredible power of habits and apply it to your work team to create more value and improve your customer experience and company efficiency. Improved customer experiences and efficiency eventually lead to stronger business performance and more opportunities for you and the members of your work team.

By reading and applying what you learn here, you will strongly influence your company's future success in a very deliberate manner, instead of just leaving it to chance.

Let's get started!

THE HABIT DEVELOPMENT PROCESS •—···

A STORE MANAGER NAMED Joe reviews his weekly customer satisfaction survey results. Compared to other stores in his region, his branch is lagging in staff friendliness. He meets with his assistant managers and challenges them to improve the level of friendliness of the staff.

When team members check in for work, they are told that they need to work on being friendlier because they have one of the lowest rated stores in the region. They aren't given much more direction than that. Most team members try to be friendlier.

The next week, the rating is slightly higher so their store is closer to average for the region. Joe checks it off his to-do list, and the assistant managers stop talking about it. They begin focusing on the next issue, cleanliness. Team members are now told cleanliness is important.

A couple of weeks later, cleanliness ratings are somewhat higher but friendliness ratings are lower. Managers tell the team members they are not putting in enough effort to be friendly and need to focus on it. The cycle begins again.

"Those team members just can't get anything right!" says one of the assistant managers.

In another area of town, but in the same region, there is another store location. This store has had the lowest ratings in the region on almost every customer satisfaction measure, and their business performance isn't any better. In fact, the store manager was recently let go and a new manager named Lisa has been assigned. Lisa is excited about her promotion to store manager and anxious to solve the challenge she is now facing.

During her first three months, Lisa and her assistant managers review customer satisfaction reports and respond in much the same way as Joe. Progress is very slow and inconsistent. Lisa's director meets with her and tells her that, while he realizes Lisa has been put into a challenging situation, he expects to see more improvement. Lisa reviews what she has done. Although her director agrees she is focusing on the right issues, he tells her that she and her team must work harder and do better.

After the meeting Lisa feels frustrated. She's been working 65 to 70 hours a week and her assistant managers are working very hard too. She's handling things the way she was taught in other stores by her store manager and director, which is very similar to Joe's approach. One of the other store managers, who enjoys higher ratings, is known as a "terror" to his staff and turnover is high. He tells his staff, "If the survey results are not high, you better update your resume." Lisa wonders if that is the only way to make improvements—through fear.

That's not Lisa's style. She says to herself, "There has to be a better way."

A DIFFERENT APPROACH

On the next Saturday morning, Lisa goes on a walk with her walking club. The topic of work comes up and she vents about her frustrations. "I'm working very hard. The whole team is.   But nothing seems to stick.   It's like we're taking one step forward and two steps back. I don't know what to do."
One friend speaks up. "I know one thing. If you keep doing what you are doing, you'll keep getting what you are getting.   Lisa, it's not about working harder, it's about taking a different approach."

Lisa replies, "That's what I've heard during my entire career—work smarter, not harder.   But that is just a cliché. It doesn't tell me what I should be doing differently."   Her friends don't have any ideas but Lisa feels that at least they care and sympathize.

She gets home and looks in the mirror.   She is pleased with the progress she has made in getting fit. Regular exercise makes her feel better about her appearance and she enjoys having more energy.   She had been trying to get fit for several years, but had challenges with consistently exercising. Then, on a recommendation, she read a book about habits. She found the topic fascinating.

After applying the principles to her workout routine and enjoying success, Lisa became even more interested in habits and how they worked. She read several books about habits. She applied what she learned to her professional life and was able to shine among her peers. That's what led to her recent promotion to store manager.

Lisa reflected back on what she'd learned about habits, about how most of the actions we take are driven by habits. Habits can be really good—they free up our conscious mind to focus on more important things and leave the driving to our subconscious mind. She reflected on the cue > habit action > reward chain and the importance of tracking results. She also thought about the importance of environmental factors on her habit development. Her fitness was due, in part, to the weekend walking club she'd started. Being around other people who were practicing the same fitness habits really helped her follow through on what she needed to do.

"That's it!" Lisa said aloud. "If I take the principles of habit development and use them with my team at the store, we will finally be able to make real, lasting, consistent progress."

APPLYING HABIT THEORY TO WORK TEAMS – THE BENEFITS

You may have selected this book because you too are struggling to make improvement with a work team of which you are a member or one you lead. The team is working very hard, but the results are not sufficient in your mind. This book applies habit theory to work teams so they may make improvements that are long lasting. It's a way to work smarter. You, your team, your customers, and stakeholders will all benefit.

Most companies approach change the way Joe did; they sometimes focus on particular areas for a period of time. This approach often doesn't work, however, because it's not quite enough. When changes are not converted to new habits, it takes conscious effort to continue performing the changed behavior. Willpower, which drives proper behavior that has not yet become a habit, is like a muscle. Extended use will make it tired and eventually it will fail.

When habits are adopted, however, the new behavior is led by the subconscious mind. The person doesn't need to think about it because it becomes automatic. When you do something subconsciously it is so much easier because it requires little focus. Remember the first time you tried to tie a shoe? If you can't recall that, maybe you can recall seeing a child struggle with tying a shoe. It's not yet a habit. It takes her full conscious concentration. In her mind she is telling each finger what to do or how to move. As an adult, tying a shoe is a habit. You don't even have to think about it at all. It does not take a great deal of effort. This is a glimpse at the power of habit.

Another good example is learning to type.   When you first learned, you had to practice every key.   It went very, very slowly and took a lot of effort.   Now that you are an accomplished typist, you merely think about the word you want to type and your fingers do it automatically. Think of people who never learned and type by hunting and pecking. They have to expend so much more effort and take a great deal more time than you would require to type the same amount.   You have a habit of typing and they don't.

When businesses make change without a solid plan to create lasting habits, they will struggle with the change like a child who has not yet made shoe tying a habit, or a person who still hunts and pecks his way across a keyboard. It takes a lot of effort and a lot of work. The result? Inconsistency. When their willpower is strong and they are committed, they do a good job. However, when they are tired, or frustrated because of the concentrated effort they have to expend, the customer experience is compromised.

One of the best symptoms and evidence of this is what you might see when you review customer contacts, comments, and online reviews. If some customers rave about having a great experience with the business while others are disappointed, you very likely have a consistency issue on your hands.

If you focus on helping the individuals on your team develop good habits, you and your team will go a long way toward achieving consistently good results. While it takes planning, effort, and time to develop habits, they are well worth it because they make everyone's job easier.   Your team members won't have to think carefully through every action because the actions come automatically.

Good habits beget good habits.   When an individual is disciplined to successfully adopt one good habit, others come more easily. This is due, in part, to the individual feeling better about himself and also recognizing and enjoying the benefit of a good habit.   Your first habit development plan will require a lot more effort than the successive ones. In a way, you are building a habit of developing great habits.

With each new habit success, your team members will actually think of themselves differently. The successful implementation of new habits will change the image of their identity that exists in their individual and collective minds. Success will be proof in their minds that they are competent in their roles. As they think of themselves as better at their job, additional habit development will become easier. They will also feel more confident.

Another benefit is that the members of your work team may apply what you teach them about habit development to other parts of their lives. That team member struggling to lose weight, or to quit smoking, or wishing to spend more quality time with her children will enjoy some success if she applies what she learns about habits and habit development to her personal life.

Through your leadership, you and other members of your team will discover the best way to add value to your customer experience. Successfully implementing habit development plans will lead to a consistently better experience for your customers. This consistency is bound to result in more loyal customers and positive word of mouth. It's a win/win for all parties involved.

INTERNAL CLIENTS/CUSTOMERS

If you lead a team that supports other parts of your organization and have internal clients, know that all of this still applies. For simplicity, this book primarily references external customers. However, you can easily translate and apply this to internal clients. All of it is relevant and fully applicable.

THE PRICE

You are probably excited at the prospect of making real, positive improvements to your customer experience. You should be. Just remember that there is no free lunch. To enjoy these benefits requires some effort on your part and some resources for the team. Let's take a few minutes to briefly tally up "the bill" you will need to pay before you enjoy the benefits.

There are several key elements to team habit development. We'll touch on many of them here. The remainder of the book will provide the additional details you need to put all the elements to use.

1) All the elements of habit development are important

When you engrain a new habit, you are actually making physiological changes to the brain. Some people may use an analogy of "rewiring the brain". Making a significant change such as permanently adopting a new habit requires a lot of effort and several factors working together in unison.

The approach we will take throughout this book accounts for these factors. There will be times when you will read something and think the suggestion is extreme. You may not agree that everyone on the team needs an overview of how habits work. You may question the need for rewards, even small ones, and also feel that the very specific tracking of habit performance is overdoing it. You may think the focus on the habit is too great, with too much discussion about it at team meetings. You may not like the idea of being a leader who needs to be super-picky when people miss practicing the habit, and dislike the need for you to call it out every time it is missed by one of your team members. There are other details in this book you may be tempted to discount as "overkill".

Yet, these details work together to make the habit successful. The approach is to use so much commitment and effort that resistance to the habit will be completely overcome.

Once you and your team have implemented several successful habits, you may experiment with backing off on the effort a bit. However, it's important to keep a close eye on the results. If they are not what

13

you've been enjoying, reinstate the elements of habit development you reduced.

For now, if you are committed to imbedding successful habits in your team members, it is important to put aside concerns that this is too much work and effort.

In his book, *The Story of You*, author Steve Chandler gives fantastic advice about how to overcome a problem.   This perspective may also be applied when attempting to accomplish anything.   In regards to how to solve a problem, he writes, "Overwhelm it.... Take massive action from a wild, high-energy state that dwarfs the problem and overwhelms it. Be inappropriate to the problem... Do not take the appropriate amount of action. Take action that is absurdly disproportionate to the problem. Embarrass the problem. Knock it out of the universe. Smash it, slaughter it, and atomize it with crushing action. Go crazy on it and beat it to a pulp."

That is exactly the approach we will take here. We are using just about every means possible to establish an important habit with your team members. If you completely follow everything outlined herein, you will overwhelm bad habits and firmly establish new, great habits.

If it were easy, all your competitors would be doing it.   Since you understand the importance of habit development and its benefits to your team, you are willing to put in the necessary effort. As a result, you will enjoy a competitive advantage.

It is worth the effort.

2) Select the right objective that will create the most value for your customers

As the team leader, you will determine the optimal objective for your habit development efforts. This is a strategic function. As leader of the team you are the person to identify the important "what" the team should be doing.

The team may become very proficient in creating and implementing habits, but if the habits they develop don't really add much value, it is all wasted effort.

Your first task is to figure out what improvements the team may make that will create the most value for your customers, taking into account the cost and effort of making the improvement. This requires thinking though the experience your customers have with your business. It involves various types of simple secondary and primary research and conversations with customers and team members. In the next chapter we'll cover this in detail. When you have completed this task, you will be able to determine what the team should focus on improving. When they successfully build habits that lead to improvement in the area you select, your customers will benefit.

3) Team members must be knowledgeable about habit theory

You are not incorporating just one habit into your team, you are doing something much more than that—you are building a process for habit development that will lead to continuous improvement. Put another way, you are not building a widget, you are building a factory that effectively creates widgets. The widgets are various habits and the factory is the habit-building process your team will adopt with your leadership.

For team members to buy in and commit to the habit development process, they must have a solid understanding of how habits will benefit them and the team, how habits are developed, and all the necessary elements of successful habit development.

This is why the team needs this knowledge before you begin to implement your first habit development plan. Without the knowledge, they will not understand the steps of the process and why each step is important. With the knowledge, they will be much more likely to commit to the habit development plan. Their commitment is a key to habit development success.

In addition, they may apply this knowledge to their personal life and develop personal habits that will make their lives better. This is a very nice benefit you will be providing to them.

4) A group of team members must be heavily involved in designing the habit development plan

If you have a small work team, you will get everyone involved in designing the habit development plan. If the habit will apply to more than 10 people, you will likely select a smaller group to develop and help implement the plan.

There are a couple of good reasons to involve team members in developing the plan. First, they do the work every day and are, in many ways, the experts. Leveraging their knowledge when the plan is developed will lead to a more realistic plan. The other reason is that their involvement will lead to a much higher degree of commitment, which is critical to success.

If you have a smaller group designing the habit and they are well respected members of the team, their commitment to the plan will be contagious.

Think of the team attitude as a flowing river. Can you move a boat upstream, against the current? Yes, you can, with a great deal of effort. However, if the current is flowing in the right direction you will be running the boat downstream. You will go much faster with less effort. When you deeply involve team members in the habit development plan, you will be setting yourself up for an easier downstream journey.

5) Set specific goals and milestones

A goal is important because it immediately aligns the team to work together for a specific purpose. The goal is the destination. It defines success. It serves as the ultimate target for everyone on the team.

The goal needs to be specifically defined so everyone is clear about exactly what is expected and by what date. The goal should be a challenge to the team, but at the same time the team should believe it is achievable.

Ideally, when goals are defined, the team is told why they are important. This "why" can be very motivating and it also helps the team push through barriers and resistance to success.

Milestones are steps to the primary goal. Milestones are important in marking progress and preventing the team from feeling overwhelmed. These milestones should be clearly aligned to the main goal. The timing of milestones may be a bit flexible, especially as your team implements its first habit. After a few habit development executions, the team should have a pretty good feel for the timing of milestones and adjustments will be less necessary.

6) Make sure the team defines a specific cue

All habits must be triggered by a cue.

A cue is an event that reminds the subconscious mind to perform the habit.

The cue may take many forms. The cue must be perceived by one or more of the senses . It may be a visual cue in that, every time the cue is seen, the person performs the habit. It may be an audio cue. Some habits may be triggered by a certain odor or taste. Feelings may also trigger a habit.

The cue of a customer approaching a register may trigger the habit for the team member to greet them. The sound of a clock chiming the top of the hour may trigger a manager to complete a cleanliness check of the restaurant. The smell of burning food triggers the habit to turn off the toaster oven. A sour taste of something that should be sweet will trigger the person to stop eating it. The feel of a warm salad plate will trigger the team member to find another plate that is cold.

Some of the best self-improvement habits are triggered by thoughts. A person striving to be more positive uses a negative thought to trigger a *but it could be worse if...* thought. The thought of a looming deadline may trigger someone to take action on a project.

If the cue is vague and not well defined, the chance of it triggering the desired habit is greatly diminished. Therefore, when the team defines a cue, it must be clear and it should ideally trigger the habit every time the cue appears.

7) Expect to make a small investment in rewards and other items

We will cover the four basic types of rewards later in the book. Some of these rewards won't cost anything and could be as simple as personal pride in a job well done. Others will generate a cost of some kind. If a team member earns a bonus break for consistently following through on habit actions, someone else will need to be paid to do the work they would have done. If you provide a bonus food item, the food cost and labor to produce the item will be an expense.

The materials you will need for your habit development plan will be few, but important. Reminder signs, notes, and cues may require paper, poster board, and markers. The habit development action plan and habit tracking sheets may be printed. You may need to invest in a small digital clock.

Based on your plans, you may choose to invest in equipment. Our base example, covered later in the book, involves installing an "Available" light at each cash register station. You may develop a special app for team members to use. However, in most cases, you won't need to make investments of this type.

8) Be obsessive about tracking habit performance

Measuring performance is important for three reasons. The first is that measuring performance is the only way of knowing if you and your team are making progress toward your objective. You may feel like you are doing a good job, but until you measure, you don't really know.

The second reason measuring performance is important is because it will allow you and the team to diagnose breakdowns in the habit development plan. If plan follow-through is lacking in some way, you may review your tracking measurements for patterns. These patterns may suggest an adjustment you need to make in your habit development plan. In many cases, you may uncover a barrier the team had not considered. With this knowledge they can develop a contingency plan to work through the barrier. Without the benefit of measurement, the team may not have recognized the barrier.

The third, but perhaps most significant reason that measuring performance is important is because it makes a great accountability and motivation tool. Awareness that team member performance is being observed and tracked will help them get through resistance to performing the habit action.   They realize that, if they fail to follow through with the habit, it will be noticed.   It adds a higher level of importance to what they are expected to do. This may often be the tipping point between success and failure.

9) Be prepared to have uncomfortable conversations

Some of your team members will quickly support your efforts to introduce great habits to the team.   Others will be resistant. For the habit development plan to work and for you to be able to provide consistent improvement, every member of the team must adopt the habits consistently.   You will likely need to have uncomfortable conversations with some team members along the way to persuade them to participate.

This requires spending time and talking through the reasons the team is developing the habit, how habits work and how the team's habit development plan leverages that, and the importance of the team member's role in the team success.   Of course, you could just tell them to follow the habit development process without such a discussion, but you will likely find this isn't very effective.

Later in the book you will learn tips on how to handle challenging team members and overcome some of the objections they may raise. If you are a leader who avoids confrontation, you will need to get more comfortable with it if you want to see your team enjoy habit-building success.

10) Be very particular and picky

As a leader, you must require strict adherence to the habit development plan. Following the plan 80% of the time isn't good enough.   To build the consistency that you want, and to make the habit quickly become engrained in the team culture, everyone will need to follow the plan every time the cue presents itself.

As the team leader, you need to be prepared to remind team members every time they fail to follow through on the habit action when the cue appears.   Some team members may feel you are being too picky and strict.   It may feel that way to you too. However, the quickest way to develop great habits is to exercise them every time they are triggered by the cue. The quicker the team members develop the habit, the quicker it will be performed subconsciously by them. When it is subconscious, it is automatic and requires little perceived effort.   This makes their job easier and provides for a better customer experience. Your strictness actually benefits the team members, although they may not always understand or recognize this.

11) The management team must be fully committed and lead the way

This book features an entire chapter about the importance of leadership in team habit development. As the team leader, you are the key to success or failure. After you and the team work together to develop a solid habit development plan, your actions and conversations in support of the plan will make it a success. If you follow the steps outlined here, if your plan is not too ambitious, and if you make adjustments to the plan along the way based on how well it is working, you will be successful.

Other leaders on your team must all be fully supportive as well. From an accountability perspective, it is often a good idea to assign the ultimate responsibility of a task to one person. You may choose to be this person. Conversely, you may designate one of the other members of your management team to lead your efforts. This person may be the one to research and identify the best objective for the habit development project, and they may meet with the team members who develop the habit action development plan. When it comes to execution, however, the management team must project a united front, with every manager taking a strong role in supporting the habit development plan.

Everyone must be involved in pointing out habit misses, in having uncomfortable conversations with team members who are not following the plan, and in communicating, tracking, and rewarding. The management team must be 100% committed to the plan from the very beginning. If you don't have support at the top, you will find it very difficult to implement your plan.

12) The approach must always come from a place of good intentions

Whether the coaching is coming from you, other managers, trainers, or accountability partners, it should always be done in the spirit of trying to be helpful with only good intentions. Some people might be tempted to use the habit development process as an opportunity to put others down who are not successfully developing the habit. Everyone is different. It will come more naturally to some and less to others. Regardless, the approach from management and accountability partners should be that feedback is solely for the purpose of helping team members improve and that there are no ulterior motives.

Always keep in mind that the objective of the habit development plan is what the team is working to achieve. All conversations and decisions should pass through this filter to make sure all efforts are aligned and effective.

Now that you know what will be required, are you ready to begin? Great! Before we get into habit theory, let's shift our minds to strategic thinking and first determine what we want to accomplish with our habit development plan.

SUMMARY OF CHAPTER 1:

- Habits are powerful tools that may be used to improve work teams, drive consistency, and help make tasks easier to complete.
- Leveraging habit development with work teams will allow them to create more value and a better experience for their customers.
- The benefits come at a cost. Habit development requires commitment and effort from management and the team.
- Twelve key aspects of work team habit development:
    1) All the elements of habit development are important.
    2) Select the right objective that will create the most value for your customers.
    3) Team members must be knowledgeable about habit theory.
    4) A group of team members must be heavily involved in designing the habit development plan.
    5) Set specific goals and milestones.
    6) Make sure the team defines a specific cue.
    7) Expect to make a small investment in rewards and other items.
    8) Be obsessive about tracking habit performance.
    9) Be ready to have uncomfortable conversations.
    10) Be very particular and picky.
    11) The management team must be fully committed and lead the way.
    12) Always coach from a place of good intentions.

DETERMINE WHICH HABITS YOUR TEAM SHOULD DEVELOP •····

THERE ARE LITERALLY HUNDREDS of great habits your team may develop; some will have a much greater impact than others. Since new habits take time and effort to develop, it is best to invest time up front to determine which habits will help your team add the most value.

At the same time, your first few habits should be habits that are not going to be overly challenging to your team. Remember that you are not only developing new habits, but a continuous improvement process so your team may always focus on getting better.

Experiencing success in developing their first few habits will give your team confidence in both the process and themselves.

So your objectives in this stage are to:

- Identify habits that will create the greatest possible value
- From among these habits, select the one that will be the least challenging for the team to adopt

Habits that will create value may be broken down into two categories:
- Habits that enable your company to provide better quality service or products to your customers
- Habits that make your company become more efficient so you may offer your product or service at a lower price or delay a price increase if there is pricing pressure

UNDERSTAND THE NEEDS OF YOUR CUSTOMERS AND WHAT THEY VALUE

Let's assume that you are in a very competitive environment and the service or product you offer is not much better than your competitor's offering. One way to gain market share is to improve the value of what you offer. Improving value means offering a better, faster, more convenient, or less expensive product or service. We'll address "cheaper" a little later when we discuss becoming more efficient.

The best way to do this is to find out from your customers what you should improve. If you have internal business partners you support, you can think of them as your customers in this exercise. All of this still applies.

What feedback do you receive from them now? What are the most common types of complaints?

Talk with your customers at the end of their experience with your business. The key question to ask, worded this way, is, "What one thing could we do to improve your experience (or this product)?" Make a note of it.

Probe further if additional explanation would be helpful. For example, if the customer said, "I just wish your cashier was friendlier," ask specifically what they could do to come across as friendlier. Ask your customer, "If you were coaching the cashier you had today to be friendlier, what would you tell her to specifically work on? Smile more? More eye contact? More small talk? A better tone of voice?"

Another question to ask is, "What one thing could we improve that would lead you to more enthusiastically recommend us to family and friends?"

Talking to your customers directly is the best way to gather the feedback. You have the ability to ask clarifying questions and, as a bonus, they will understand that you are truly trying to improve their experience with you.

Now you know what to focus on.

What if there isn't anything obvious? What if your customers seem generally satisfied and can't think of anything to do to improve your business? Unless you have nearly 100% market share for your trade area, you can still improve and generate more long-term business, and, in the process, ensure you will be able to keep your current customers coming back.

If the approach of just talking with your customers isn't easily done or if you want to go a different route, you can survey them.

In either case, start by analyzing your business in a more sophisticated way by process mapping the customer experience.

PROCESS MAPPING YOUR CUSTOMERS' EXPERIENCES

Let's begin by process mapping your customers' journey in purchasing and using your product or service.

Why do we start with process mapping? Process mapping your customers' experience will open your eyes to opportunities for improvement.

Step back and think very broadly about what your team is trying to accomplish for your customers. Think about the benefits you are providing.   For example, if your company sells ice cream bars on the beach, you could think of the work you do as "provide a refreshing treat to satisfy hunger needs and a need to cool people off in a setting that will create a great, lasting memory of enjoyable times with friends and family."

You aren't just selling ice cream bars.   You are satisfying hunger and contributing to an emotional experience. Thinking about it from this perspective reveals even more options to improve your service or product.

Fully immerse yourself in your customers' perspective. Before you put pencil to paper, begin thinking through the answers to these questions:

- What prompted my customers to first think about needing my product or service?
  - o   Was it due to a physical cue (e.g., hunger, pain)?
  - o   Was it due to an emotional need (e.g., need for affirmation, need to overcome fear)?

- How did my customers first hear about my company?
  - o   Did a friend tell them about it?
  - o   Did they read about it in a blog post?
  - o   Did they see advertising on TV?

- What made them think of my company in association with the need for the product or service I offer?
  - o   Did they mentality link a positive past experience with my company in meeting their need?
  - o   Did my advertising make them more aware of their need and prompt them to take action?
  - o   Does my company own a spot in their consideration set for meeting this need?

- What prompted them to contact me, walk into my establishment, or do business with me in another way?
  - Did the need drive them to make a decision to take action and my company's offering was chosen?
  - Were they surfing the internet when they saw my ad, remembered a need, and took action by clicking to my site?
  - Had they decided earlier in the week to take care of that need with my company based on their weekly routine?

- In their contact with my company, what was the first thing they saw or heard?
  - What impression/emotion did they feel when they visited my website or walked into the door of my business?

- What steps did they take through the purchasing process?
  - What was their cost in terms of money, effort, and time?

- What steps did they take in using my product or service?
  - What was their additional cost in terms of money, effort, and time as they used the product or service?

- What benefits did they enjoy along the way, physically, mentally, and emotionally?
  - How did using my product/service make them feel?
  - How well did it satisfy their needs?
  - In retrospect, did they feel good about doing business with me? If so, why? If not, why not?

The above questions will put you in the right mindset to map your customers' experience.

On a sheet of paper write down the very first step of your customer experience. It should be the initial prompt that causes your customers to realize they have a need they want met. It may be feeling hungry, seeing an advertisement, running out of something, or a myriad of other reasons. Note that there may be a couple of different first steps, depending on your customer. If so, list these vertically on the left side of the page. Draw a square around each of these.

Then write down the next several major steps in the process until you are at the very end. Put a box around each of these. It's entirely possible you'll need additional sheets of paper.

Let's go through a very simple example. Imagine you have an ice cream wagon on the beach. Here's how your process map might look:

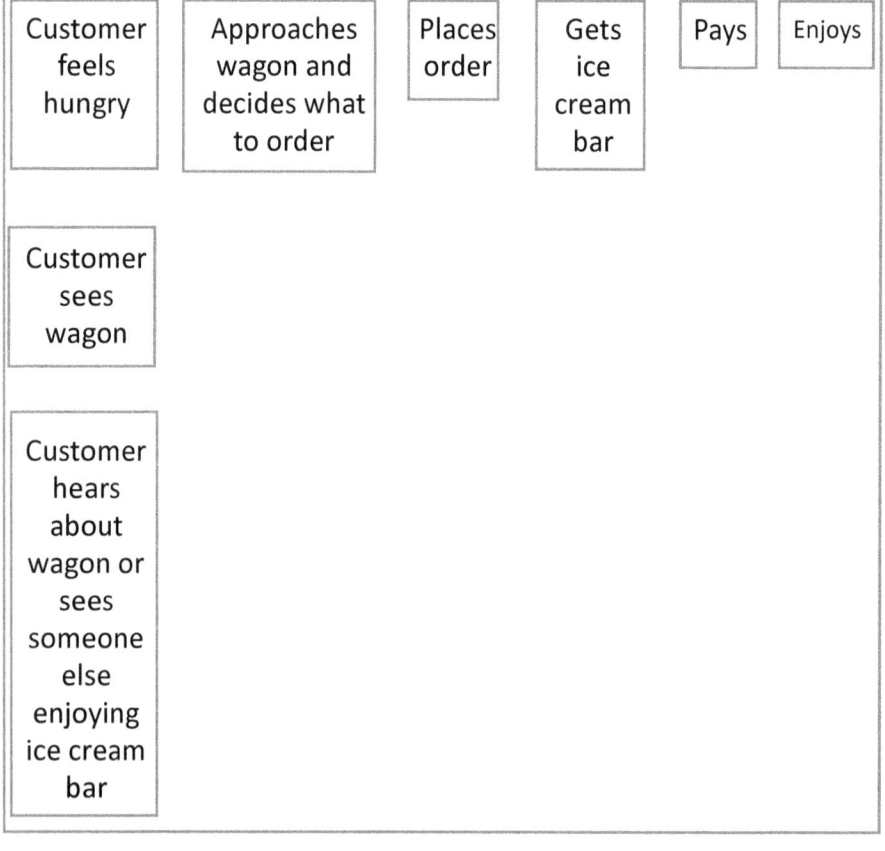

Now we are going to examine each box for opportunities to improve the experience. Below each box (or maybe on another sheet of paper), we'll make a list of the components of each step.

Customer feels hungry—there really isn't anything we can do to impact this step

Customer sees wagon—we have control over this. Here are some examples:
- Location of the wagon
- Size of the wagon
- Signage on the wagon

Customer hears about the wagon. Yes, we can impact this:
- Provide such great customer service and value that we earn positive word of mouth (the best advertising possible)
- Invite customers to tell their friends about us
- Set up a Facebook page
- Provide a frequent buyer card for locals who frequent the beach

Approaches wagon and decides what to order:
- Ensure that the wagon is very clean and in good repair
- Team member makes eye contact and smiles at customer
- Create an inviting, approachable space
- Post a sign that clearly indicates what is available (including the prices)
- Team member greets the customer when he/she gets close enough and asks what the customer would like
- Team member ready to recommend favorite if customer not sure and asks

Places order—again, we have a lot of control over this sub-experience:
- Team member interacts in a positive manner
- Team member accurately captures order
- Team member announces total so customer can get payment ready

Gets ice cream—this covers everything to do with the product:
- Product is available
- Product is right temperature
- Product wrapper is clean
- Product wrapper is still sealed
- Product is of high quality
- Napkins are available

Pays—this is more than just taking the money:
- Team member makes eye contact and smiles at customer
- Customer preferred payment method is accepted
- If paying in cash, correct change is returned and bills are dry
- If paying by debit card or other means, the technology authorizing payment works quickly and flawlessly
- A receipt is offered
- Customer is sincerely thanked for their business

Enjoys—the ideal outcome:
- The customer enjoys his or her ice cream
- The customer records in her mind the memory of enjoying an ice cream bar on the beach with her family. Maybe it's the first time her child has had an ice cream bar, making the memory even more special
- The customer feels good about their service experience
- The customer tells others about their great experience
- If there is any issue with the ice cream bar, service recovery is provided in an excellent manner

While there are potentially dozens of components to each step, we are only noting the most obvious at this point.

DETERMINING THE MOST IMPORTANT ELEMENT

Now we need to evaluate each of the elements. To do this, you'll want to compare your business to the ideal customer experience. What would an absolutely perfect experience look like?

To consider the ideal customer experience, you probably have good judgment yourself. If you are not sure, think of your strongest competitor and "shop" them to get a feel for what parts of the experience they perform best. Then challenge yourself to think of a way to top that.

Now that you have very high standards of the ideal customer experience in mind, it is time to rate how well your business performs for each of the components you have listed. Keep this scale in mind:

- 10 – There is no possible way to improve this component
- 9 – Perfectly executed as designed, every single time
- 8 – Executed perfectly almost all the time
- 7 – Executed perfectly at least half the time
- 6 – Not always executed perfectly, but no major errors; this is the level of performance that most customers expect
- 5 – On rare occasions, execution is flawed to the point that it creates dissatisfaction with your customers but most of the time it is solid performance
- 4 – Problems crop up from time to time due to poor execution, although there are still occasions of solid performance
- 3 – Execution is rarely perfect; customers would say it is not as good as other places they visit
- 2 – Execution is often poor
- 1 – Proper execution is almost non-existent

You may have noticed that the scale is focused on consistency. This is perhaps the biggest challenge facing work teams today—consistently delivering great results. Establishing good habits with your team members will go a long way toward improving consistency.

Are you still not sure how to rate your performance? Another option is to do a "local measure".

If there is a big problem, you can have your team members start to track it. For example, if you think frequently running out of change is an issue, keep track of how often it happens so you can really determine if it is a consideration.

By now you have identified the aspects of the experience that have the greatest opportunity for improvement. These are the lower rated items on your list. But this is only half of the equation. Now you need to determine which of these will have the greatest impact on your customers' overall experience.

PRIORITIZING THE OPPORTUNITIES

Being very efficient at something is not of any value if that something is not significant or important. Always focus first on being effective (doing the important things right) then strive to be efficient (doing things with the least amount of effort and resources possible).

You can gather data points from a number of sources to help you determine which improvement area you focus on will lead to the best outcome for your customers.

As mentioned before, talking with customers allows you to better understand their needs and perceptions. If you tried and weren't successful in identifying opportunities before, try again using the list of the lower performing items you identified. You can make a list of four to eight of these items on a sheet of paper.

Intercept customers and tell them your team is working on a project to improve the customer experience. Show them the list, telling them these are the areas of improvement you are thinking of focusing on and ask them to identify the one or two they feel would be most beneficial to them if the team made improvements.

Then take the opportunity to probe and understand what the customers' expectations would be of this part of the customer experience. You might ask how a company like yours could go "above and beyond" in these areas. This will give you some very helpful information that will be useful later on as you work on specific habits.

SURVEYING YOUR CUSTOMERS

You may also consider surveying your customers.   This can be done via pencil and paper, but a better approach may be to use a survey program on the internet such as SurveyMonkey. Tools like this allow you to quickly program a survey and retrieve results swiftly at a nominal price.

There are other books about how to put together a good survey, so we won't go into a lot of detail here, but let's outline how this type of survey might be written.

Let's assume this survey will not be a tracking survey, but just a one-time survey to identify the best, most important opportunities for improvement for your business.
- Open with a statement thanking them for taking the survey and telling them you appreciate the feedback and that you'll use it to make improvements in your business
- Ask them to compare their overall customer experience at your business with other businesses they visit
- Do the same with each major aspect of the experience
- If they indicate that you are not as good in one area, ask an open-ended question about specifically how your company might improve
- The last question on the survey should ask what one aspect of the experience they recommend you improve

Here's an example survey for our ice cream wagon.

Thank you for completing this short survey about our ice cream wagon.   Your feedback will help us improve future customer experiences.

1) Compared to other ice cream wagons or a similar type of vendor you've ever bought ice cream, sodas or snacks from, how would you rank us?
    o The very best
    o Better than most

o A little better than average
o Average
o Not quite as good as most
o One of the worst
o The very worst

For what reasons did you answer this way?

_____
_____
_____

2) How do we compare based on the following?

	The very best	Better than most	A little better than average	Average	Not quite as good as most	One of the worst	The very worst
Ease of finding wagon	☐	☐	☐	☐	☐	☐	☐
Ease of making choice of what to purchase	☐	☐	☐	☐	☐	☐	☐
Friendliness of Staff	☐	☐	☐	☐	☐	☐	☐
Accuracy	☐	☐	☐	☐	☐	☐	☐
Speed of Service	☐	☐	☐	☐	☐	☐	☐

Quality of Product	☐	☐	☐	☐	☐	☐	☐
Price	☐	☐	☐	☐	☐	☐	☐
Ease of paying	☐	☐	☐	☐	☐	☐	☐

3) If we were a little better than average or less than average on any of the above, please tell us specifically how we could improve to make your experience better in the future. You may want to describe other great experiences you've had at other similar businesses:

_____

_____

_____

4) Considering every part of your experience in doing business with us, what is the most important thing we should work on improving?

_____

_____

_____

How do we get customers to take this survey if it is online? One way would be to print business cards with the website address and a place to write a code when they complete the survey so they may exchange the card for a free ice cream bar. At the end of the survey there is a code they write on their card.

On the page where you provide the code, you may also provide a link to like your Facebook page or ask them if they would like to provide their email address to receive special offers and news in the future.

The information you gather from the survey would be very helpful in determining what you and your team should focus on to make improvements.

OTHER WAYS TO HELP PRIORITIZE

There are other data points you should consider to determine what is most important to your customers. These include:

- Observe your customers interacting with your business. Look carefully at their body language. What part of the experience seems to make them happy and relaxed?   During which parts do they look disappointed or annoyed?
- Ask your team members what they think they do that customers really like. What parts of the customer experience do they think the customers don't enjoy as much?
- Look for secondary research on the internet. Google key word phrases about your business (e.g., "ice cream wagon most important").   You may have to wade through several sites before you find something useful.
- While you are on the internet, check to see if there are any reviews or comments about your business or similar businesses (even if they aren't even in your area). These comments can shed some light on what customers value the most.

By now you should have a pretty good idea of what your business needs to work on to improve the customer experience.

Pick the top actions you and your business can take to add value to the customer experience. Do this by rating each action on a 10 point scale (1 = not very impactful at all, 10 = extremely impactful). The next step is to determine the level of difficulty for each.   Also do this on a 10 point scale (1 = very easy to implement, 10 = very challenging to implement).   Select the top actions first based on impact, and then sort these based on level of challenge, beginning with the easiest first. Save the list because after you tackle the first couple, you will go back and select some of the more difficult actions that are very impactful.

What if you determine that the best thing you can do to add value is to be more efficient in your operation so you may lower your price or at least keep future price increases at a minimum?   It's time to do another process map, this time from the company operation perspective.

PROCESS MAPPING YOUR BUSINESS PROCESS

Now we'll process map the procedures your company goes through to deliver product and/or service to your customers.   This will likely include several steps that your customers never see, but are nevertheless critical to the customer experience and may be a source of increased efficiency.

A variety of departments need to work together to deliver your product or service. These departments include operations/production, marketing, finance/accounting, and human resources.   If you had responsibility to improve the company as a whole, you would want to examine each of these departments.

Chances are, however, the improvement project you are working on concerns only one of these teams or a subset of one.   This being the case, you will only need to process map the processes your team participates in, either as a doer of the work, a receiver of inputs, or a disseminator of outputs. As you complete the exercise below, ignore the parts of it that may not apply to your work team.

Before putting pencil to paper, let's think about the process and begin to identify the various elements.

You can begin by consulting your customer process map.   For almost every step on that map, you can identify ways your company contributes to it. As you think through the various procedures, you will want to determine who does each step, what they need in terms of input (information, product or supplies, service or assistance from someone else) and timing.

You may be surprised when you think of how many different processes your company engages in to serve your customers. That's because most of these processes are performed on "auto-pilot". Many of your processes are done a certain way just because "We've always done it this way." This further illustrates the power of habits, good and bad.

- How do we market our product or service to our customers?
    - What are the various ways we use to market to customers?
    - What is the production process behind each?
    - How do we determine the objective of each message?
    - What are the necessary steps to develop the creative (the wording, audio, visual, etc.)?
    - What are the steps required to schedule the marketing efforts?
    - How do we make sure all the different marketing efforts work together and complement each other in a strategic way?
    - How do we evaluate the effectiveness of each marketing effort?

- How do we provide a place for our customers to do business with us? This could be a physical location like a store, a virtual location like a website, or some other location.
    - If we are in a building, what are the steps we must take to maintain it in good working order? How do we make sure it is clean and inviting to our customers?
    - If we operate from a website, how do we retrieve what customers might put into it? What is our process when we respond to customer orders or inquiries? How do we keep it up-to-date? How do we keep it accurate? How do we make sure it is working properly all the time? How do we get it fixed if there is a problem?
    - If we travel to our customers, how do we get there? If there is a route in visiting our customers, how is the most efficient and effective route determined? What is the process to update it as new customers are added? How do we maintain the company vehicles?

- What is our process to make sure that our team members who interact directly with our customers represent our company well? This interaction may be in person, over the phone, or through the internet.
    - How do we make sure they are fully trained and up to speed on the latest information they need to know?
    - How do we make sure they are in a good frame of mind and are very customer focused?
    - How do we make sure they represent our company well, either in dress, vocal quality, or written skills?
    - How do we provide feedback on an ongoing basis to ensure company performance standards are maintained and even improve over time?

- What are the processes involved when customers use our product or service?
    - How do we handle assisting customers with selection?
    - How do we fill orders once a customer makes their selections?
    - How do we package the orders in an efficient manner?
    - How do we provide information that customers request or need?
    - How do we follow up with customers after the sale to make sure they are satisfied or find out if there is any other way we can assist them?
    - How do we process payments and collections (either at the time of payment or as an accounts receivable process)?
    - How do we handle returns? What is the process for restocking and refunding?
    - How do we gather feedback from our customers on a regular basis to make sure we continue to meet their needs with the services or products we offer?

- How do we minimize costs for our company?
    - o Do we look at other potential vendors from time to time to make sure we are maximizing value based on our needs?
    - o Are there less expensive options available for sourcing our products?
    - o Do we outsource when it is less expensive, or manage it in house when that is the more cost effective approach?
    - o What are others in the industry (or even other industries) doing to minimize costs without negatively impacting customer value?
    - o How does our company pay its invoices? How are billing disputes resolved?
    - o What is the process taken to ensure our company receives what it is paying for?
    - o Are we spending money to provide something to our customers that they don't value? Does everything we do for our customers or provide to them add incremental value?

Many of your current processes are probably fine.   They are efficient and effectively meet their objectives.   However, there are always opportunities for improvement in some areas.   The exercise of thinking through each process will move it from something that is automatically done as dictated by habit to something you are aware of so it can be examined for improvement opportunities.

It is important to consider the implications of the hand-offs of work from another team to your team, or from your team to other teams, because these are often areas of improvement opportunities.

Now you will create a process map based on how you deliver your product or service.

We'll return again to the ice cream wagon example. To simplify the process, we will just consider the activities of the team member who works at the wagon.   Assume there is someone else who has stocked the wagon with ice cream bars. Your team member stops by the office to pick up change. There she counts it. She goes to the wagon and verifies the inventory. Then she opens for business. When her shift is over, she is relieved by another team member who has his own change bank. They verify the inventory together and she takes her money to the office.

Here's how the process map for her position might look:

| Arrive at Work | Pick Up and Verify Bank | Verify Inventory at Wagon | Greet Each Customer | Take Customer's Order | Get Their Ice Cream Bar(s) |

| Collect Payment | Keep the Wagon Clean | Call When Additional Stock is Needed | At End of Shift, Verify Inventory | Count Bank |

Next we would examine each box for opportunities to be more efficient. Below each box (or maybe on another sheet of paper), we'll make a list of the components of each step. Below is a list of a few components that might come under the first few boxes. Your list may be considerably more extensive.

Arrive at work
- Process to record that the team member arrived on time.
- Manager and supplies are present so the team member can get right to work.
- Efficient process to communicate important information to the team member (e.g. weather forecast, special events, changes to offerings or prices).

Pick up and verify bank

41

- Manager removes bank (change for the day) from the safe and gives it to the team member to count.
- Team member counts change and bills on the desk and initials paperwork.
- Money secured.
- Manager accompanies team member to the wagon.

Verify Inventory at Wagon
- Team member counts boxes of each type of ice cream bar and records them on an inventory sheet.
- Team member's inventory sheet is verified against stocker's inventory sheet.
- If the count does not match, the manager conducts an inventory and notes a discrepancy (if there is one).
- Team member uncovers the sign.

Greet Each Customer
- As soon as the team member hears or sees a customer approaching the wagon she looks up, smiles, and makes eye contact.
- She says, "Good morning, may I help you?"
- She answers questions the customer may ask.

Take Customer's Order
- Team member listens attentively to customer's order.
- Team member enters the order into POS (point of sale) system.
- Team member asks if the customer would like anything else.
- Team member gets ordered ice cream bars and presents them to the customer.
- Team member points out the napkin dispenser if she thinks the customer may not see it.

We would continue this list for all steps in the process of the team member's day.

Now we review each item and determine if there is an opportunity to make it more efficient.   We are trying to reduce the time involved, reduce the effort involved, and/or make it happen correctly more consistently.

Let's take the first one: "Process to record that team member arrived on time." How is this done now? Is this done with pencil and paper? Is the manager just making a mental note? Does the system allow the team member to "clock-in" or record their arrival electronically?

If the manager is just making a mental note, do we need to set up a formal system? It depends. If team members always arrive on time then a formal system may not be necessary.

However, if the lax tracking of arrival time results in team members arriving late and the ice cream wagon not always opening on time, a more formal system should be considered. After all, we are not serving our customers well if we don't open on time and may lose some business.

How do we know if it is an issue or not? We have the manager (or someone else) purposefully and accurately track the arrival time of all team members for several days. If team members are arriving late and it is impacting business, a more formal check-in system may make sense. At that point, you'd investigate different options to accomplish this.

Let's take one more subset of checking in: "Manager and supplies are present so the team member can get right to work." What supplies are needed to be prepared? Are they always ready? If not, what is the root cause and what process can we set up to make sure the team member is not delayed because her supplies are not available?

To determine if this is an issue or not, we do another "local measure". These are simple tick sheets that track whatever you want to track. This is a quick, easy to identify opportunities. The tick sheet may be used after you make a change in the process to make sure your new process solves the problem.

Here's an example tick-sheet we may use for supplies for several days or a couple of weeks. The team member puts a mark in the box if an item is missing or not readily available.

Pen	~~HHH~~ ~~HHH~~ II	Radio	
Paper		Crash sheets	
Towels	~~HHH~~ II	Gloves	I
Receipt paper		Trash can	
Rubber bands	I	Rain Gear	IIII

If the above trend continued with different team members on different days, it might tell us that we need to make sure we have pens and towels available for team members and determine why the rain gear keeps going home with other team members.

Pens? Is that really a big deal?   The answer is "yes" if it delays your team member and causes customers to wait or results in lost sales, or if it creates frustration for your team member, causing her to be less friendly when assisting customers. In a process, missing something minor may have a large impact.

You may also consult the internet about some of the processes to identify opportunities. Google "How to be a faster cashier" and compare what you find to how your team members do their job.

Process mapping and examining it takes time and effort, but if it's never been done before or not done for a while, you are bound to identify opportunities to be more efficient.

Get your team members involved.   With so many items to investigate, ask them what they think are the greatest opportunities for improved efficiency.   What frustrates them? What slows them down? What creates problems for them?   Focus on these areas first and you may quickly uncover some opportunities.

After process mapping and investigating the sub-steps, you will likely have an extensive list of possibilities. Now you will review them and evaluate them based on potential benefit to improve efficiency and level of difficulty.   Rate each on a ten point scale based on these two factors (1 = very small impact on efficiency, 10 = very big impact on efficiency and 1 = very easy to implement, 10 = very challenging to implement).   You may wonder why we are focusing on efficiency rather than effectiveness. We've already focused on effectiveness when we determined that the most effective, value adding activity we can do for our customers is to be more efficient so we may lower our prices or minimize future price increases.

Now look at the items you rated as having high impact and identify the one or two of these items that would be easiest to execute.   Think of these as your productivity improvement opportunities.

PRIORITIZE YOUR LISTS

If you've followed along, process mapping the process from both the customer and business perspective and drilled down on all the sub-steps, you'll likely have a list of improvement efforts you would like to work on.   Some of these will result in an improved experience for your customers, while others may impact efficiency, which also benefits the customer.

In the next chapter, we'll begin to get team members involved in the process.

CHAPTER SUMMARY

- First determine the most effective actions you may take to improve the customer experience then focus on how to efficiently perform these habits.

- The best way to understand your customer needs and how well your company is doing in an effort to meet these needs is to talk to your customers.

- Process map your customer experience to really understand it from their perspective.
  - Break up the customer experience into several steps and clearly define what happens in each step.

- If possible, shop your competition to evaluate what they do better than your company.

- Observe your operation and rate each step on how well you do compared to your competition.
  - Consider surveying customers to get their perspective of how you do vs. other options.
  - Ask your team members to list your company's greatest opportunities for improvement.
  - Look for reviews about your business and other similar businesses on the internet to see what customers seem to value the most.

- If you decide it is best to focus on efficiency to help maintain low prices for your customers, process map your business process.
  - Closely examine each step in the business process for opportunities to enhance efficiency.
  - Use local measures (e.g., tick sheets) if necessary to better understand opportunities for improvement.

- Prioritize everything you have learned and select one or two key improvement areas you would like your team to work on that are important but also relatively easy to improve.

o It is important that you have success with the first few habits so you can establish a continuous improvement mindset with your team members.

PROVIDE TEAM MEMBERS WITH HABIT DEVELOPMENT KNOWLEDGE •····

NOW THAT YOU HAVE strategically determined which improvement areas you'd like your business to focus on, it is time to get your team members involved.

Making change will go so much smoother if those involved have some input regarding the change and how it happens.   With your list of areas of focus, you have established the "What actions we are going to take."   As a team, your team members will develop the "What habits we should develop to best accomplish those actions."

Before this work begins, however, it is important that you provide some knowledge to team members so they may be able to do a great job of it.

If you have a small team of less than 10 people, ideally you would have a team meeting and get everyone involved. If the team is larger, you may announce to the team that you are beginning a continuous improvement process and you would like some team members to form a committee to develop the plan. This committee may be ideally made up of about four to eight team members, but any number you choose is fine.

You will want to set up two meetings. The aim of the first is to review the goals of the improvement effort and to educate team members about habit development. The second meeting is intended to actually plan the habits the team will practice. We'll cover that in the next chapter.

If you go the committee route, know that when you begin developing habits among the team members, it will be necessary to train everyone on the team about habit development. This training will lead to knowledge about habits and a much smoother and successful habit development process.

THE INITIAL MEETING

Always keep top of mind that, when you are motivating your team to make a change, you should use every opportunity to talk about what is in it for them. A good way to start is to review the state of the business. Talk about how your company is doing and the realities of the competitive environment. You are likely in one of three situations:

1) Your company is struggling and needs to turn things around or you may not survive long term. Team members may need to realize that, if business doesn't improve, jobs may have to be eliminated.
2) Your company's performance has been pretty flat, neither gaining nor losing ground. As a result, there is little opportunity for team members to advance within your company.
3) Your company has been doing well and is a strong competitor. In this case, you want to continue to offer better value to your

customers. This will create more opportunities for team members in the future.

Team members need to understand why it is important for the team to focus on making improvements based on your current situation.

Next, briefly review the steps you took to determine the most effective actions your team can take to add value to the customer experience, whether it is improving the experience or working on efficiency to lower or maintain prices.   If you mapped the process, you can share it with your team, but don't get too bogged down in reviewing it. Your objective here is to show the team that you really put a lot of thought into coming up with your list of actions and to communicate to them why they were selected.

Ask for their feedback and be open to listening to different points of view. Ultimately, however, the decision about what to focus on lies with you as the leader of the team. Not everyone on the team may agree with the areas selected for improvement, but at least they should have an understanding of and respect for why these areas were selected.

The team's role in this planning is to determine the specific habits the team will adopt to accomplish improvement in these areas.

REVIEWING HABIT THEORY

For the team to develop a process to implement great new habits, they first need to have an understanding of how habits are developed and work.   In the rest of this chapter, we'll review an outline of what this session might look like.

To make educating your team easier for you, we've created a PowerPoint presentation you can access at WorkTeamHabits.com using passcode 11302.   This PowerPoint presentation follows the outline below and may be used as you train your team about habit theory. This is designed to be interactive so you'll see questions throughout that will keep your team engaged as you review it.

What follows is a suggested script you might use. You may ask the questions included as rhetorical questions or actually solicit answers and drive more engagement.

SCRIPT FOR EXPLAINING HABIT DEVELOPMENT

Why We Are First Learning About Habits

Now that we've reviewed what we want to accomplish, as a team we will figure out how we will make these improvements.   Before we do that, however, I want to introduce you to an important tool that will make our improvement efforts easier and longer lasting. This tool is habit development.

The information I'm about to share with you will not only help us here at work, but you can also use it to make your personal life better and easier. In fact, most of the examples we provide will be person-based so you can easily benefit personally from what you are about to learn. I think you'll find it very interesting.

How Do Habits Benefit Us?

Habits make your life much easier. If it weren't for habits, you would be exhausted from focusing and paying close attention all day long. Let's take a moment to talk about one example.

Many of you backed your car out of your garage or parking space this morning. While you may have felt like you were focusing, you really weren't thinking through all the steps in detail. What were those steps? There is a fair chance that you don't recall doing many of these specific actions you executed just a few hours ago:

1) Lifted the handle to open the car door.
2) Swung it open, making sure you didn't hit it against anything.
3) Sat in the driver's seat.
4) Put on your seat belt by reaching over to the left, pulling on it, and snapping it into place.
5) Took the key out, lined it up with the ignition, and slid it in.
6) Put your foot on the brake. Turned the key just the right amount. Let go of the key when the car started.
7) Put your hand on the gear shifter and moved it just the right amount to the reverse setting.
8) Looked back over your shoulder to see if there was anything behind you.
9) Slowly eased your foot off the brake as the car went into motion.
10) Monitored the speed, making sure you were moving at a good pace, but not so fast you risked losing control.   Eased off the brake as needed, just the right amount to do this.
11) The entire time you were backing up, you looked behind you to make sure no car, person, or animal passed into your desired path.   If you spotted something, you immediately pressed the brake.
12) As you backed up into the street, you turned the wheel in the opposite direction you wanted the front of the car to face.   You turned the wheel just the right amount to back safely into the street and straighten out.
13) You shifted your car into drive, made sure the road in front of you was clear, and proceeded.

This is a 15 second process you go through each day, yet you are barely aware of all the steps. You likely do it thinking about something else and are not very conscious of any of it. Yet, you are able to do it safely, day after day, year after year.   Because you have a habit of doing all these steps, your mind doesn't have to work very hard and you benefit by doing a rather complex set of steps quite easily.

Take a moment and recall when you first learned to back a car out of a garage or parking space and how you had to focus on every little detail. What was that like? Remember how nervous you were the first time you drove? You focused on every step and likely had someone talking you through them. You likely didn't back up smoothly, it was probably more of a stop-start-stop-start jerking motion. Your heart was beating fast and your breathing was fast and shallow. Your hands may have been perspiring and there may have been a knot in your stomach.

Today, when backing up, you rarely have these feelings and if you do, chances are it's because something unexpected happens (like a dog suddenly running across the driveway behind your car).

Our brains are designed to be very efficient. They focus resources where they are needed and also look for opportunities to do things automatically and subconsciously. This is because your conscious mind can process 40 bits per second, while you can subconsciously process 11 million bits per second. When your brain is able to, it moves as many actions as possible to be directed by your subconscious mind. This frees up your conscious mind to focus on the things that are really important.

Habit Development Principle #1: Habits help us become more efficient by shifting attention and effort to the subconscious mind where the task can more easily be handled.

This serves you well in many cases, but can also be detrimental to you. It all depends on the habits you develop.

GOOD HABITS AND BAD HABITS

If you really put your mind to it, you could list several hundred good habits you have. What are some examples? Some are very simple like brushing your teeth before bed, looking both ways before you cross the street, or putting a napkin in your lap when you sit down to eat.

You may be aware you are doing them in the moment, but you don't have to think through the steps. You just do them.

You also may have some bad habits. Biting your nails when you are nervous, drinking too much when you are feeling low, or turning on the TV when you have other things you should be doing are just a few examples.

If all our habits were carefully planned, life would be great. We'd only have good habits and they would all be very efficient and helpful. However, many of our habits were adapted without much thought. One day we did something a certain way, the next day we may have done it the same way again and a pattern started to set in. Each day we did it the pattern in our mind became even stronger.   Scientists have found that habit formation actually changes the neuron connections in our brain. Every time you adopt or change a habit, you are rewiring your brain!

Habits develop naturally, whether you intend for them to or not.

Bad habits are usually developed without much thought. Someone seeks instant gratification and trades a great future benefit for much less benefit in the moment.

You spend time aimlessly surfing the internet because it feels fun and engaging. After 30 minutes of surfing you haven't really learned anything useful with your time. Instead, you could have spent quality time with your child reading a book, which creates a closer bond between you and your child and helps reinforce an enjoyment of reading that will serve your child well for the rest of his or her life.

Sometimes bad habits lead us to do things that will cost us in the future.

You reach for a 10th piece of chocolate because you are nervous, not hungry, and it makes you "feel better" for a few minutes. Meanwhile, your commitment to eat healthier has just been set back.   Will that one action ruin your health? No, but this action, along with others like it, will add up and impact you negatively.

People who text while they drive likely didn't purposefully decide to do that. Chances are that, one day, while they were driving, they received a text and thought a textversation with a friend would be enjoyable. *Just this once,* they may have thought as they drove and texted. Arriving safely, the seeds of a new habit were planted. Over the course of the next several weeks they text and drive more and more until it becomes a habit so strong that even the bombardment of public service announcements they hear every day and an awareness that it is risky behavior can't change the habit. Eventually, they will quite possibly end up in an accident and hurt or kill themselves or others, just because a bad habit developed. Their entire life is changed forever.

On the other hand, when we adopt a good habit consciously we benefit. This is because these habits are almost always a result of higher level thinking. You realize that, to have great future benefit, you might have to put forth some effort or delay gratification in the current moment.

Exercising is a great example of this. Few people begin a successful exercise regimen without first focusing on the benefit it will bring in terms of better long-term health and more energy. Keeping the benefits in mind, you exercise one day and then the next, and then the day after that.   Although there is always some effort involved, once you've been exercising for several weeks without fail, it becomes a good habit that will benefit you greatly in the long term.

Another good habit is to save money.   To do this, most people need to have a budget, which is just a plan for allocating money in a way that a portion of income is left over at the end of each month for savings. People who develop a habit of creating and following a budget have to sometimes delay gratification. Maybe their entertainment budget for the month is all spent so they will need to wait for that new movie to get to Netflix to see it. But the benefit of the security of having savings for emergencies or retirement is enormous in comparison.   Will compromising and going off budget break the bank?   No, not due to the cost of one movie ticket.   However, it will potentially "break the bank" because it starts the person down a road of the habit of making exceptions to the budget.   Eventually, they find they are living paycheck to paycheck.

If we are aware of the power of habits and how they work, and apply this knowledge purposefully, we can benefit ourselves greatly. We can make good choices, select the habits that would be most helpful to us, and then follow a process to develop those habits. They will eventually be done subconsciously, with little effort, yet we will continue to enjoy the benefits.

Habit Development Principle #2: Good habit development is a purposeful process.

THE HABIT EQUATION

All habits follow a three step process:

Cue >> Habit Action >>   Reward

A cue is what triggers the habit.   If you have a cat or dog and feed them canned pet food, there is a good chance that they come running when they hear the can opener.   That is their cue.   The habit action is to run to their bowl.   The reward is their enjoyment of the food.   If you like animals, this is a great example to help you recall the three step process.

Let's talk though a couple more examples.

Your cue is the clock or end of a TV show telling you it is time to go to bed.   You go into the bathroom and brush your teeth (habit action). The reward is reinforcement of your self-belief that you are a hygienic person.   In addition, you've reduced the chance of getting cavities and your mouth feels fresh and clean.

You are driving and come to a red light. The cue is the light turning green. Your action habit is to press the accelerator. Your reward is to move closer to wherever it is you are driving to and to avoid the frustration that would have been taken out on you by the drivers behind you if you had not gone.

Here's an interesting one. Assume your spouse appreciates it when you leave him or her a note in the morning before you leave for work. Each morning you get up and go for a jog. Your cue to write the note is walking in the door from your jog. Your reward is the good feeling you get for doing something you know your spouse appreciates.

However, one morning it is raining and you decide to sleep in. What are the chances you'll remember to write the note? You would likely forget. Why? Because the cue of you returning from your jog never happened, so the habit action of writing the note was never triggered.

Now think back on the example of feeding your pet. If your electric can opener wasn't working one day and you had to open the can with a manual opener, you would likely have to call your pet to come eat, because she would not hear the regular cue.

Habit Development Principle #3:   All habits must be triggered by a cue.

CONSISTENCY IS KEY

In developing habits, achieving consistency is of primary importance, especially in the beginning.

Imagine you own several acres of land and the land has a very slight downward slope running from the north to the south.   Now imagine that to the north there is a mountain with melting snow.   Water begins running down the mountain and rolls right over your land.

Let's assume you notice the water running onto your land and you figure out that it would be beneficial to you if the river ran in a straight line across your land in a certain path. Because there is not an established path, it would not take very much work. You would simply dig a small trench across your land so that the water would follow it. This trench may only need to be a few inches deep.   Renting the right equipment, you might be able to dig this trench yourself in a day.

You'd watch it carefully over time to make sure the river stayed on your path and you would make corrections as needed.   This would get easier and easier because over time the river would continue down the path and would grow deeper, greatly increasing the chances of it staying on this path.   You might have to check in on it daily at first then on a weekly basis, and then even less frequently. Eventually, you wouldn't need to give it another thought because it would be so well established. As the owner of the land you would benefit because a little effort up front established the path the river will take for years to come.

Developing a new habit works the same way. It takes a lot of attention and effort early on until it becomes established.   The key is consistency—repeating the habit consistently will make it easier and easier. If the development of the habit isn't consistent, it will take a lot of effort. It's like the river—if it follows the path every day, it gets established pretty quickly. If it goes off path some days, it takes constant effort and a lot more time to establish it.   Just like habits.

Consistency also helps you keep the momentum going. With momentum you can quickly build on your success each day.   If you lose momentum (consistency), it will take a lot more effort to get back up to speed.

Habit Development Principle #4:   Habits are built quickest when you consistently practice them every day.   This builds momentum.   The less consistency the longer it takes to establish a habit and the more effort it takes.

Given all this, how difficult should the habit action be?

MAKE IT EASY

In the book *Mini Habits: Smaller Habits, Bigger Results*, author Stephen Guise makes a great case for using the approach of beginning with very easy actions to get habits started. Instead of planning to start a grandiose habit (like running 5 miles per day), you would just establish a habit of putting on your running clothes and going for a short run. You are "successful" as soon as you hit the pavement. Most people will end up running further distances over time, but you overcome the psychological barrier by giving yourself credit for just getting in motion.

If putting on your running clothes and beginning to jog is too hard, simply make your habit to put on your running clothes each day. Most people can at least do that. Then you define that as success. Most people, while they are dressed, would go ahead and begin jogging.

The point is that, after several days of very consistently practicing a minihabit like this, it will eventually become pretty engraved into your daily routine. At that point you may set a little higher goal like a specific distance. Never set a goal so high that you fail. It should be simple enough that you rarely have an excuse not to do it. This approach works because it keeps you consistent. And consistency is the key to developing any habit.

Habit Development Principle #5: When planning the habit action, consider making it a very simple action initially so you can focus on building consistency.

IMPORTANCE OF TRACKING

When planning your new good habit you need to develop a plan for tracking progress. Consistent tracking of your habit development performance will greatly increase your chance of success.

First you have to clearly define success. Exactly what is a successful habit action? Is there a quality component to it? For example, if your habit is to greet each customer who walks in the front door, is it important that the greeting be enthusiastic and genuine? If possible, determine a pass/fail standard. However, if this is not possible, besides determining if you completed the habit action you'll need to evaluate habit action quality.

Your tracking system is dependent on the type of habit you are developing. If it is a habit action that is to happen once a day and there is no quality component (e.g., you either do it or don't do it) you can adopt the Jerry Seinfeld method.

Jerry Seinfeld's goal is to write some new comedy material every day. Each January he puts a large annual calendar on the wall. For every day that he writes some comedy material, he puts a big "X" over that day. Over the course of several weeks you would see a chain of "X"s. Seinfeld's goal is not to break that chain of "X"s.

That is one very visual method that may work well for you.

Another way to track is to create an excel sheet with the dates going down the left side. In the second column, you keep track of how many days in a row you were successful with your habit action. If you slip, you begin again the next day and try to break your consistency record (highest number of days in a row so far). You could track this just as easily on a sheet of paper.

Some habits happen multiple times a day. These are a little more complicated to track. If it is not too challenging, you can track it on a tick sheet. Each time the habit action cue comes up, you'll note whether or not you followed through on the habit action. You may track daily performance as a percent successful. If the cue came up 10 times and you followed through with the habit action 7 times, then you achieved 70% success that day. On future days you'll want to try to beat this percent.

In other cases with a habit that happens many times a day, it may not be easily possible to track success in the moment. In these cases you may want to give yourself a letter grade. "A" means you felt you were always successful in following through with your habit action, "B" means you only missed once or twice, "C" more often and so on. If you never or rarely followed your planned action habit, you'll want to grade yourself an "F".

If you think you can accurately judge an entire day, give yourself a grade for the day. If you are unsure whether you can accurately assess your performance, consider giving yourself hourly grades. This provides the additional benefit of reminding you of the habit every day or every hour.

Another point to consider is who does the tracking. Since some of the habits you develop will be team habits, you will want to designate someone to keep track. It may make sense for this person to be the team leader or manager. This is especially true if there is a quality component to your action habit.

Your tracking should be reviewed on a regular basis. It may serve as an intrinsic reward in the form of pride in achieving a certain level of consistency. It also serves as a feedback mechanism that points to a possible need for adjustment. If you discover, through your tracking, that you are not following the habit action consistently whenever the cue is supposed to trigger it, you may need to revisit your habit plan and see if any adjustments need to be made.

- Is your habit purposeful enough? Is it being given enough attention and support?
- Do you have a clear cue to trigger the habit action? Is there a better cue to consider?
- Is the habit action step simple enough? Are you being too ambitious? Is there a better minihabit you should consider trying until you build consistency and momentum?
- Is your reward plan solid? Do you need to add additional rewards from other categories of rewards?
- If you are overcoming a bad habit, do you have a clear good habit to replace it with? Is this good habit triggered by the same cue and likely to result in a comparable or better reward?

- What is causing you to be inconsistent in following through with the habit action? Do you have contingency plans for these situations?

Habit Development Principle #6: Tracking habits action performance is critical to the success of new habit development. Develop a tracking plan and decide how often you will evaluate and adjust performance.

GOALS

Now that you have measures, you will need some goals.

These goals should be SMART:
- Specific: Specifically what you are trying to accomplish. In some cases, it may be useful to state who is completing the task, when they are completing it, and where they are completing it.
- Measureable: Use the measures you have just developed and tie your goals to these. Tying a goal to a measurement makes it clear and allows you to objectively determine when the goal is achieved.
- Attainable: Goals should be a stretch, but must be attainable. If the goal is too challenging, you risk giving up or losing interest.   If the goal is too easy, you risk missing your full potential. If you are unable to believe that the goal is possible, you may want to be less ambitious.
- Realistic: Goals should align with your long-term vision and help advance you toward it.   In addition, you should value the goal enough to put in the effort it will take to achieve it.
- Timely: Goals should have set deadlines or milestones for progress. Without a deadline, there is not a sense of urgency and progress will slow way down.

Let's look at an example:

Not a SMART goal: I will exercise more.

SMART Goal: I will jog two miles at 5am on Mondays, Wednesdays and Fridays at a speed of a 10 minute mile or better. I will add a half mile to my run each week for the next 16 weeks until I am running 10 miles three times a week.

An easy way to measure your progress system is to use the habit tracking measures that you previously developed.

Let's pause a moment and define some terms we are about to cover. Defining them up front will make them easier to understand:

- Objective: what you are ultimately trying to achieve. One example of an objective may be to lose 10 pounds.
- Goal (sometimes called ultimate goal): what you are doing to achieve that objective. A goal may be our previous example of jogging three times a week, 10 miles per run.
- Milestone Goals: easier goals than your ultimate goal. These are steps along the way.   This is the 2 miles the first week, 2.5 the second week, and 3 miles in the third week. Each of these would be a milestone goal.

You may have an objective you want to achieve.   However, you may not want your objective to be the goal you focus on daily.

The best measures on which to base goals are the measures of things you can directly control. Your best, focused goals should be on consistent completion of the habit action.

For example, you may have a vision to lose weight and you initially consider setting a goal of losing 10 pounds in the next five weeks by eating healthier.

However, there are several factors that impact weight loss.   Every person's body is different and reacts differently to diets; otherwise there would be one diet that everyone would use. Instead there are many diets because some work for some people but not for others.

When you have a goal like losing weight, you want to consider that there are two factors involved:

1) If the habit action you developed is effective (meaning if it will achieve your goal)
2) If the habit action is consistently performed

You may be very consistent in performing your habit action, but if it is the wrong action, you may not achieve your goal. You may adopt a habit of dieting during the week and splurging on the weekends to maintain motivation. While you may be able to consistently perform the habit, you likely wouldn't lose any weight.

Conversely, you may select exactly the right habit (3 meals a day, 10 bites per meal), but not be able to consistently complete it. In either case, you would not succeed. If your goal was to lose weight, you might just give up altogether and never know why it did not work. If, instead, your goal was to succeed with the habit, you could master the habit and then determine if it was effective based on whether it helped you achieved your vision.

With habit development, you have goals and milestones. Goals are what you are trying to achieve. A goal might be how consistent you wish to be with your habit. Milestones are steps toward that goal. They are mini-goals.

Think of your goal as the top of the mountain. This is the level of performance that, if maintained consistently over time, would make your vision a reality.

However, the top of the mountain may be a daunting goal to many, especially if they are looking at it from the base of the mountain. Some people may be motivated by it, but most may feel it is not achievable. This is where milestone goals come into play.

You may decide that your ultimate goal is 95% consistency in completing the habit action, but the milestone goal for the first week is 60% consistency. As you successfully complete the current milestone goal, you will want to raise the bar toward your ultimate goal.

Each week the milestone goal is raised and over time you eventually achieve the 95% ultimate goal. In the mountain climbing example, this is like the "daily goal" for the mountain climbers, it is the next campsite a little further up the mountain. Although you are aware of the ultimate goal up front, this weekly goal should be the primary focus. In some situations you may have an increasing daily goal rather than an increasing weekly goal.

Habit Development Principle #7: Your habit development plan should include an objective, SMART goals, and SMART milestone goals.

REWARDS

Rewards are important too. Rewards are the motivation to complete the habit action. Without some kind of reward, it is challenging to adopt a significant new habit.

Rewards come in many forms. There are two basic kinds of positive rewards: extrinsic and intrinsic.

Extrinsic rewards come from outside of you. Examples include money, treats, and participating in activities, like going to the movies.

Intrinsic rewards are rewards within you. Examples include pride, satisfaction, and feeling good for doing something nice for others.

In our previous examples we saw various types of rewards:
- Pets get an extrinsic reward in the form of food when they run to the dish after you've opened a can of their food.
- Leaving your spouse a note results in an intrinsic reward of feeling good because you did something you know he or she appreciates.
- Your reward for brushing your teeth is both intrinsic (feeling good that you are a hygienic person) and extrinsic (your teeth feel clean).

Intrinsic rewards are most effective when you pause and focus on them. If your intrinsic reward is a sense of pride in a job well done, you should pause and allow yourself to feel that after successfully completing a good habit. Make that feeling a reinforcement of your positive self-image. This is useful for two reasons. First, you deserve to enjoy the reward and, second, it increases the value of the reward, making it even more effective in the future.

While we usually think of rewards in the positive sense, either extrinsic or intrinsic, we should broaden our definition. Another common type of reward is the avoidance of punishment. These may also be done on an extrinsic and intrinsic basis. Some examples of rewards that are really avoidances of punishment include:
- You press the accelerator on your car when the light turns green to enjoy an extrinsic reward (i.e., avoiding others honking at you).
- You drive slowly through your neighborhood to avoid hitting someone's pet, which would make you feel terrible. Your reward is intrinsic because you are avoiding feeling bad about yourself for hurting an animal.

In summary, we have four types of rewards we may consider when designing a new habit:
1) Positive intrinsic
2) Positive extrinsic
3) Avoidance of negative intrinsic
4) Avoidance of negative extrinsic

Habit Development Principle #8: There are four types of rewards: positive intrinsic, positive extrinsic, avoidance of negative intrinsic, and avoidance of negative extrinsic.

MULTIPLE REWARDS

When we design a new habit we'd like to adopt, we need to carefully consider the reward. It is natural to focus on the positive extrinsic reward because that is the easiest and most obvious. However, for some habits, a positive extrinsic reward won't always work. Sometimes it must be combined with other intrinsic rewards.

How many people have begun dieting, reached a plateau in losing weight, and stopped dieting as a result? Successful dieters understand this and mentally prepare themselves for the possibility of several weeks of no progress. Their reward isn't just losing weight but the self-satisfaction of being persistent and consistent with their dieting.

A person who is dieting could set up a reward plan that takes into account all four types:
1) Positive intrinsic: reminds themselves how good they feel about their level of self-discipline every day that they stick to their diet.
2) Positive extrinsic: losing weight and advancing toward their weight loss goal.
3) Avoidance of negative intrinsic: avoid feeling the frustration with themselves they'd feel if they didn't follow their diet.
4) Avoidance of negative extrinsic: avoid paying a friend the $10 they promised them for each day they went off diet.

Some habits are so easy that they may not need a reward after they are well established, or the reward may be minimal. Think about a reward structure described above. This is necessary and important as you get started.   But after you've been practicing good eating habits for a long period of time, it becomes part of your self-identity. You see yourself as "a person who consistently makes healthy food choices." As you continue to eat healthy, you enjoy an intrinsic reward of reinforcing your positive view of yourself.

Habit Development Principle #9:   You may plan on multiple rewards early on to reinforce the positive habit. As the habit becomes embedded, you can scale back the rewards.

CHANGING BAD HABITS

The first nine principles work well when establishing new habits. But how do we overcome bad habits? Why are they so hard to change?

Let's go back to our river example. Imagine that you bought several acres of land that has water flowing through it. The water has been running through your new property as long as anyone can remember. But instead of a planned path, this river formed its own path based on the terrain at the time it began. As the water flowed, it found the lowest level and followed this south. The path is similar to many other rivers, following a path that curves back and forth. If you've ever looked out the window of an airplane, especially in the western part of the United States, you've likely noticed these rivers.

Since it's been established for a while, the path has grown deeper and deeper, forming a substantial riverbed following the same path. Over the very long period of time, a canyon formed following the river. If you wanted to purposefully straighten out the river, you could. Changing the path of a river is not impossible, but it does take a great amount of effort. The longer the river has been flowing in that manner the greater the required effort. It could potentially cost hundreds of millions of dollars and take several years.

Think of this path as an unintended habit that has been in place for a long period of time. It will be challenging to change it. There are two approaches you could take. You might try to straighten out each curve like this:

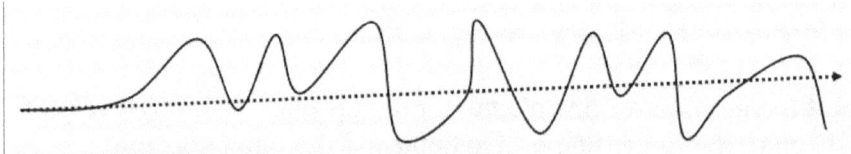

That would require a lot of work, cutting into the canyon walls in several places. It would be a massive effort.

Another approach would be to develop a totally new path:

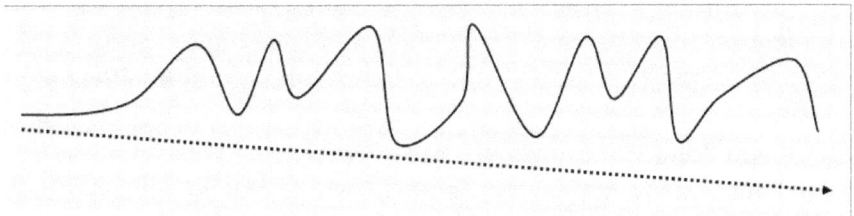

This approach would be easier. You would establish a path in another place and then direct the source of water into your new path. The old river path is so very well established that it would take a lot of work to change it or stop the water from flowing through parts of it.

The same applies to habits. Instead of trying to change a bad habit or stop it, you will have more success if you come up with a replacement habit.

For this new, good habit to replace the bad habit, it must have two things in common with the bad habit: It must be triggered by the same cue, and it must have a reward that meets the same needs as the bad habit.

Here is an example. Assume that when you get home from work every day you have a need to de-stress. Your cue is walking in the door; your bad habit action is to immediately turn on the TV and watch anything that happens to be on and snack on chips. Your reward is stress relief.

Recently you have developed a desire to live a healthier lifestyle. You come up with a great idea for a new, good, replacement habit.   Your new habit will be to take a walk after work.   You decide that the cue is arriving home.   Your habit action is to put on your shoes when you arrive home and head out the door. You don't necessarily have a planned distance; you just walk until you feel sufficiently less stressed.

If you do this every day after work for several weeks it will become a habit. You have the same cue (arriving home stressed) and the same reward (calmness to overcome your stress) but the action is totally different (putting on shoes and walking instead of eating chips while watching whatever happens to be on). You have not only begun to defeat a bad habit, but you've also created a great new, healthy habit.

What if you don't want to walk? You may come up with another replacement habit. Maybe this habit is, instead of watching whatever is on TV, purposefully recording good, uplifting or interesting TV shows. Instead of having chips in your pantry, you keep grapes or apples in your refrigerator. Now when you arrive home stressed (your cue), you watch the productive, recorded show and eat a healthy snack (your new habit action), and you get the same benefit of de-stressing (same reward). In addition to de-stressing, your reward is feeling better about yourself for doing a healthier action.

Contrast this with not coming up with a replacement habit but instead just trying to stop the bad habit. You tell yourself you won't watch TV when you get home. However, when you get home the cue triggers you to watch TV and eat chips. With some willpower, on some days you might be able to resist. But even on the days you do resist, you'll miss out on the reward and still feel stressed. This will make it more and more challenging each successive day because your need to de-stress is not being met. Chances are you will fall back into your old habit.

To overcome a bad habit you really need to create a replacement habit.

Habit Development Principle #10: If you are trying to overcome a bad habit, you should create a new, good habit to replace it. The good habit should be triggered by the same cue and provide the same psychological reward as the habit you are replacing.

HABIT CONTINGENCIES

Assume you've carefully planned a habit following all the principles we've covered. You experience a few days of success but then a "barrier" to your habit comes up. So you make an exception and intend to go back to it the next day. Now you have lost consistency and momentum. If the "barrier" occurs for several days, you will lose all momentum and must exert a lot of effort to get your habit development back on track.

How can you combat this? We need to develop habit contingencies. Habit contingencies are your plans to overcome possible barriers to your habits. Identify what may happen, and then plan on how you will handle this. Since your planning is done when you are calm and rational, you will be able to overcome the tendency not to follow the habit if the barrier arises.

Let's return to our replacement habit of going for a walk instead of watching TV and snacking on chips when you get home from work. What happens if it rains? If you don't plan for that, you could quite possibly think that you've been doing well with your new habit for a few days and with the rain you can't walk, so today it would be okay if you watched TV and had chips. That would result in lost momentum and your new, good replacement habit may be at risk.

If you take time to make a contingency plan, you can overcome this temptation of returning to your bad habit, and instead keep the momentum going. What are some options for when it rains?
- You can go to a local mall or big store and walk around there.
- If it's not raining too hard, you can grab an umbrella and rain boots and go for a walk in the rain.
- If you have a gym membership, you may grab your iPod and go use the treadmill.
- You could engage in simple stretch exercises that you've already researched and know how to do.

Whatever your plan, you want to have the items and knowledge you need to be able to implement it, if necessary. For example, if you planned to give yourself an option of doing any item on the above list, you would need to identify a mall and know the hours it is open; you would need a big umbrella and rain boots; you would need a gym membership with your membership card handy; or you'd need to have a planned routine of stretch exercises.

Rain is just one barrier to developing your new habit; another could be an injury. What would your contingency be for a twisted ankle? What if you were out of town on a business trip? What if you were sick? What if you were very hungry when you got home? Make a list of barriers and options. Keep the list handy. If you get home (your cue) and a barrier keeps you from your normal habit action, immediately (without allowing yourself to think about it) pull out your contingency plan and follow it.

Contingency tip: If/Then. A simple yet effective way to think about contingencies is to put them in an If/Then format. If (barrier) comes up then I will (contingency plan). If it rains, I will drive to the mall and walk; if I am injured, I will read a book and eat fruit. Here's a double If/Then: If I'm on a business trip, I will inquire about walking in the area, but if the area isn't safe, I will use the hotel treadmill.

Habit Development Principle #11: Having a plan for habit contingencies will help you overcome barriers that might arise and keep the momentum and consistency going. Use the If/Then formula to make your plans easy to follow.

REMINDERS

Habit action reminders are always helpful. If the habit is one that is typically triggered several times during the day, reminders are extremely important if you wish to be consistent and gain quick momentum.

An example of this would be if your new habit was to smile whenever you answered the phone so you'd naturally sound friendlier to the person calling. The cue, of course, is the ringing phone. The reward is a feeling of pride that you were pleasant to the other person on the phone and this, in turn, feeds your self-image of being a friendly, corporative business partner.

Although you may remember to do the habit action of smiling when you are talking on the phone, a reminder would help set you up for success. You might use a visual reminder. This may be in the form of an index card reminding you to "smile" or a multiple cards with messages or pictures reminding you to smile. Each time you answered the phone, you'd advance to the next card. This might better help you keep it top of mind than a single reminder card that never changed. Over time, due to habits we have in regards to limiting our focus, the card may be overlooked and ineffective.

In this case you may consider other cues to add to the cue of the phone. Maybe you can change the ringer sound to something different than you are used to and you associate that sound with the habit action of smiling. You may have a small smiling toy or plush you keep next to your phone that you purposefully smile at just before you pick up the receiver.

You can combine a reminder with tracking. Get a stack of pennies and a jar. Each time you answer the phone successfully with a smile, put a penny in your smile jar. If you miss a smile, take a penny out of the smile jar. In this way, you have both a visible reminder and a tracking system all in one.

These reminders may be reduced or eliminated as you set a long track record of success with your habit development.

Habit Development Principle #12: Reminders are a good way to help keep habits top of mind. Reminders should stand out and be a "secondary cue" to trigger the behavior.

ENVIRONMENTAL INFLUENCES

Did you ever consider how much your environment influences the choices you make and the actions you take?

We are all very susceptible to the environment around us. Our environment can help us with our new habit creation, or it can serve as a hindrance. At the very least we need to understand and think though environmental influences so we may reduce the impact of the negative ones. Ideally, we can adjust our environment so it helps, rather than hinders, good habit development.

What do we mean by environment? The environment is anything outside of your mind that may be able to influence your thinking and choices. This includes:

- Other people
- Anything you may see, hear, touch, taste, and smell
- Events that may take place in your immediate proximity or things that happen elsewhere that you may be aware of

Your thinking is influenced by whatever is happening wherever your attention is focused. The TV shows you watch, conversations you have, and books you read all influence your thoughts and thus impact your progress in good habit development.

It has been said that a person is most like the five people they are closest to. If you spend your time with healthy, athletic people, chances are you are healthy and athletic. If your conversations are mostly with friends who have a negative outlook on life, you may adopt the same attitude. You tend to adopt the values of those around you, even as you influence them.

Have you ever made a New Year's resolution that you were not able to keep? Almost all of us have. Think back on the moment you went off track. What was going through your mind? Chances are it was related to an environmental factor. Were you dieting, out with friends, and they were all enjoying a delicious appetizer that you couldn't resist? Were you jogging regularly and a couple of really cold mornings kept you from going out and defeated your momentum? Were you really serious this year about not wasting so much time surfing the internet but an email from a friend prompted you to check Facebook at work "just this once" and soon you quickly found yourself back to your old habits?

The environment is a powerful force that we can often overcome when our willpower is strong, but very few people can overcome strong negative environmental influences all the time.

On the other hand, the environment can be helpful. How many exercise sessions would be successful if they only included exercising with a friend? How many times have you taken long-term positive action in your life that was inspired by something someone said? How many dieters were more successful after they threw out all the junk food in their house and replaced it with healthy options such as fruit?

The environment is too important not to consider it when you are developing your habit plan.

Start by making a list of both positive and negative environmental factors. Consider each person with whom you will come into contact. Will they be a help or a hindrance? How?
What can you do to impact that in a way that contributes to your habit development? Do you avoid some people altogether? Do you tell them about your habit project and ask for their help in a specific way? Do you "brace yourself" when you know you are going to be around them, anticipating that they may not be helpful?   Do your contingency plans include overcoming the negative influences of others?

While some people may quickly take you off track, others may be very helpful. Many people are able to succeed in establishing a new habit only when they have an accountability partner. The accountability partner is someone aware of their habit development effort. This is someone they check in with from time to time; they tell their accountability partner how they are doing. They talk about successes and failures and discuss what led to both.

Accountability partners are helpful for a couple of reasons. Discussing habit development efforts with them leads to a deeper understanding about what works and what doesn't. This understanding may be successfully applied to the person's benefit.

Just knowing you will be facing an accountability partner, and telling her how you are doing, can be very motivating. In times of weakness, you may not have the willpower to be able to follow the habit for yourself, but the prospect of having to tell your accountability partner that you've failed may be just enough motivation to help you get through the habit.

The best accountability partners are the ones who you greatly respect, who value your relationship, and understand and are committed to your goals. They are compassionate, yet won't let you off the hook if you fall short. When you fail in your habit they should be encouraging, but also point out that you can and should do better. Accountability partners who do not call you out when you fail, and help you come up with excuses, are not doing you any favours.

With a team approach to habit development, the entire work team serves as accountability partners for everyone else. This should be encouraged. It is important, however, that the attitude is "good will intended" and not a way for team members to put each other down. Accountability partners do not enjoy seeing their friends fail. They want to see them succeed. They see their responsibility of holding them accountable as something they do to be genuinely helpful, but it is not something they enjoy doing.

How can you impact your physical environment? Are there places you need to avoid? Everything starts in your mind with a thought. That thought leads to action. What environmental influences do you know might send you down a wrong path of thinking that could lead to a habit development setback? If you can't avoid or change these influences, at least anticipate them and the impact they could have on your habit development if you aren't guarded. Yes, you need more If/ Then contingency plans.

Team habit development, which is what we are about to do, actually leverages this environmental factor in a very positive way. If you are the only team member trying to practice a new good habit, it can be challenging. Imagine that you are inspired to begin a new good habit that will improve your customers' experience with your business, but all your fellow team members are still acting the same way as they always have.   You may be able to be consistent with your habit and, if you are really good, you might influence the others around you to be better.   However, that puts a lot of work on you and your willpower. If you are strong enough, you may persevere, but it will be an uphill climb.

Contrast that with another situation.   You and your team get together and develop a good work habit you all agree to adopt.   You serve as accountability partners for each other and together you create positive environmental influences (like the reminders we covered under Principle #12).   Do you understand how much easier it would be for you to adopt and stick to a new habit?   With faster, better success, you and your fellow team members will be able to adopt other good habits and soon have a very positive impact on customers' experiences with your company.

Habit Development Principle #13:   Environmental factors greatly influence your chance for success in habit development.   Where possible, adjust these factors so they may be helpful. If you are unable to change a negative environmental factor, at least anticipate it and think through how you will work through it and reduce its influence on you. When work team members develop new habits together, they can leverage their influence on the environment to their benefit.

LENGTH OF TIME TO DEVELOP A HABIT

How long does it take to develop a habit?   It depends.   If the cue is very clear, if the habit action is very easy, the reward is enticing, and you are very committed, you could develop a new habit in as few as several days.   If the habit is particularly challenging and difficult, it may take several months for the habit to be embedded.   Getting to this point may require a lot of self-experimentation with various cues, minihabit approaches, and rewards to discover the best formula for you.

Now that you and your team are up to speed on the key principles of habit development, it is time to plan our first habit development project.

CHAPTER SUMMARY

If you lead a large team, form a committee of about four to eight team members to work on the habit development plan. If your work team has 10 team members or less, involve everyone.

In your initial meeting with the team you'll want to cover these topics:
* Business conditions and why you are focusing on habit development.
* Outline how you selected the objective of your improvement efforts.
* Review habit theory so that everyone begins with the same base of knowledge.

In your overview of habit theory, you will cover the 13 habit development principles:
1) Habits help us to be more efficient by shifting attention and effort to the subconscious mind where the task can more easily be handled.
2) Good habit development is a purposeful process.
3) All habits must be triggered by a cue.
4) Habits are built quickest when you consistently practice them every day. This builds momentum. The less consistency the longer it takes to establish a habit and the more effort it takes.
5) When planning the habit action, consider making it a very simple action initially so you can focus on building consistency.
6) Tracking habit action performance is critical to the success of new habit development. Develop a tracking plan and decide how often you will evaluate and adjust performance.
7) Your habit development plan should include an objective, SMART goals, and SMART milestone goals.

8) There are four types of rewards: Positive intrinsic, Positive extrinsic, Avoidance of negative intrinsic, and Avoidance of negative extrinsic.

9) You may plan on multiple rewards early on to reinforce the positive habit. As the habit becomes embedded, you can scale back on the rewards.

10) If you are trying to overcome a bad habit, you should create a new, good habit to replace it. The good habit should be triggered by the same cue and provide the same psychological reward as the habit you are replacing.

11) Having a plan for habit contingencies will help you overcome barriers that might arise and keep the momentum and consistency going. Use the If/Then formula to make your plans easy to follow.

12) Reminders are a good way to help keep habits top of mind. Reminders should stand out and be a "secondary cue" to trigger the behavior.

13) Environmental factors greatly influence your chance for success in habit development. Wherever possible, adjust these factors so they may be helpful. If you are unable to change a negative environmental factor, at least anticipate it and consider how you will work through it and reduce its influence on you. When work team members develop new habits together they can leverage their influence on the environment to their benefit.

PLAN THE FIRST TEAM HABIT •—··

NOW THAT EVERYONE IS up to speed on the 13 principles of habit development, it is time for your work team or committee to put this knowledge to use.

Prior to covering habit development, you told your team about your business's current situation and what broad area of improvement you'd like them to focus on.   Your work team now has the task to determine the specific first habit they will develop.

Before you begin generating ideas, it may be useful to process map the specific situation you are addressing. For example, if you are working on improving speed at check out, process map this part of the broader shopping experience from a customer perspective. This process would start when the customer has the items she wants to purchase in her hands or in a shopping cart, and end when she leaves the checkout area.

Process mapping will help the team identify additional possibilities to improve this specific process from the customer perspective.

Then process map the checkout process from the business's perspective.

After everyone has gained an understanding of what we are trying to improve, you will want to begin a brainstorming session. After answering any additional questions they may have about what you've covered to this point, you can lead the team in a brainstorming session to determine what the specific habit might look like.

TEAM BRAINSTORMING

Team brainstorming is a great way to generate ideas, it leverages the brain very effectively. The left side of a person's brain is analytical, while the right side is creative. Without engaging in a brainstorming exercise, the team may attempt to develop and debate ideas at the same time. While seemingly efficient, this actually stifles creativity.

The best way to generate great creative solutions is to first develop a long list of creative ideas. This is best done without judgment at all and should be very free flowing. Withholding judgment makes it safe for people to speak up about any idea they have, even if it is quite a bit different than conventional approaches.

Even silly ideas can lead to great breakthroughs. A story was told at a conference about how a brainstorming session that seemingly bordered on silliness led to an ideal solution to a problem.

The problem was that too much snow was gathering on top of high power lines. The weight of the snow caused the power lines to break, resulting in outage for the customers of the power company. In addition, repairs were costly and took a lot of effort. What could be done to get the snow off the power lines before it built up so much that it snapped the power lines?

The brainstorming session began. One thought was to have people go up the power poles and shake the power lines to get the snow to fall. Then someone said that, instead of having workers go up poles, they should entice bears to climb up them and the bears could shake the power lines.

"How would you get the bears to go up the poles?" someone asked.

Another team member piped in, "We could put fish at the top of the poles and the bears would climb them to get to the fish."

"How would you put the fish on the top of the poles?" someone else inquired.

Another team member said they could use helicopters to place the fish at the top of the poles.

Someone asked how they could secure the fish to the top of the poles so that air from the helicopter blades wouldn't blow the fish down.

Then came the ultimate solution: "Hey, we could just fly helicopters over the power lines to blow the snow down before it builds up too much!"

This story is a great illustration of how brainstorming works when people feel free and safe to offer very creative ideas.

Throughout this habit development process you will want to utilize brainstorming at different steps. Here are some brainstorming guidelines:
   1) There are no bad ideas! This is the first rule of brainstorming because it is the most important.
   2) When brainstorming, everyone is using the right side of their brain. They should be as creative as possible.
   3) During a brainstorming session there should be no judgment regarding the feasibility of the ideas. It's fine and good to ask inquisitive questions that may lead to other ideas, but no one should say, "That wouldn't work because…"

4) Participants need to resist self-judging when generating ideas.
5) All ideas are captured.

Before beginning the brainstorming, it is a good idea to review the ground rules. You may even post them so they are visible during the session.

You'll need some supplies for the brainstorming session:
- Index cards and pens (consider different colors)
- A flip chart with several pages
- Masking tape so you can tape flip chart pages to the wall
- A timer (or you may just use your phone)
- A few pages of small, round stickers

The world is made up of introverts and extroverts. Because introverts like to process their thoughts before speaking them aloud, they may not get as involved if you jump right into verbal brainstorming. The best way to leverage the creativity of both introverts and extroverts on the team is to conduct the brainstorming session in two parts.

Before you begin, talk about the objective of the brainstorming. This first brainstorming session is to focus on specific habits the team may develop under the area of focus. It is usually a good idea to have this visible.

For example, if the area of focus is to improve the speed of cash out in a store, the team would brainstorm habits that would contribute to this. You could write this as the objective in statement or question format. Here are a couple of examples:
- Brainstorming Objective: Improve the speed of cash out
- How can we improve the speed of cash out?

Begin by handing out index cards and pens to everyone. Some people may be even more creative using different colored pens or index cards.

Set a timer for two minutes and challenge everyone to come up with three or more ideas. Now set it for three more minutes and ask the team to dig deeper and individually write three more creative ideas.

Your team has spent five minutes brainstorming in total and you may have as many as six ideas from each team member. Your team is off to a great start.

Now go around the room and ask each team member to read out their first idea. Write this on a flip chart. With each idea, ask the group if they had a similar idea or any ideas on how to build on that. Keep going around the room in this manner until you've captured everyone's first idea. Then do another round with everyone's second idea. This goes on until all ideas have been captured.

By the time you are done you should have multiple flip chart pages posted around the room.

Ask if there are any more ideas. Give the room a full 30 seconds of silence before concluding that you've finished the brainstorming session.

Now it is time to evaluate the ideas.

Now the team will shift gears and switch to logical, left brain thinking as they evaluate ideas. The challenge is to come up with the best solution to meet the objective. It needs to be the best, not necessarily the most creative or most practical.

One of the best ways to evaluate ideas is the pros and cons approach. This approach involves making a list of all the reasons this idea meets the objective, and another list for the reasons it might not, or issues or costs it might create.

If you go back to your flip chart you'll likely have more than a dozen potential ideas. Try to combine them when possible. There may be two ideas that are essentially the same but are just stated in a different way. Combine those. There also may be cases of one idea being a sub-idea of another. Combine those as well.

If you now have a manageable number of ideas to engage in a pros and cons discussion, you may begin. If you still have too many ideas you'll need to narrow the list further.

One way to do this is to hand out the sheets of round stickers and give everyone the same number to place on ideas on the board. They may place multiple stickers on any items they feel strongly about. After everyone has placed their stickers, select the top ideas with the most stickers.

Now it's time for the pros and cons exercise. Select one idea and ask the group to name reasons why it is a good idea and meets the objective. It's important you keep the team focused on the objective. Some really great ideas may be proposed, but if they don't meet the objective they should be saved for another discussion on another day. Once the pros list is exhausted, develop the cons list. Why might this idea not achieve the objective? What additional resources might be required? How might it impact other aspects of the customer experience, or other parts of the company?

If the cons are slow in coming, you will want the team (or maybe specific members) to play the "devil's advocate" and argue against the idea. They may personally favor the idea, but they are still challenged to come up with reasons why it may not work. If it is a popular solution, the team can discuss how these limitations might be overcome.

Let's go through an example. We'll use the objective of increasing the speed of service at checkout. Let's assume one of the popular ideas is to open an additional register as soon as there is more than one person in line.

The pros:
- Faster check out for the customers in line.
- Less chance of losing sales to customers in too much of a hurry to stand in a longer line.
- The customers may recognize that this store "values my time."

- Customers may spend more time shopping since they know they will be able to check out quickly.

The cons:
- Additional labor would be required. If people are being pulled from stocking to open a register, you'll have to make up that stocking labor eventually. This will increase the store costs and lead to higher prices for customers.
- There is some inefficiency to the stocker who keeps getting pulled to work on register. Every time he goes back to stocking, he has to readjust to resume working where he left off.
- Customers waiting in line less time may make less impulse purchases.

Not all pros and cons are equal.   Some are much more important and impactful than others.   After listing and reviewing the pros and cons the team may come up with some kind of "score" for the idea.   It may be a number on a 1 to 10 scale, with 10 being an idea that clearly meets the objective with no downside.   A 1 means it falls short of meeting the objective and/or the cons make it very unappealing.

You and the team would go through each idea in a similar manner. After doing that, pick the top two or three scored ideas and have a final discussion before agreeing on one.

This approach—brainstorming followed by evaluation—is a tool you will want to use throughout this process.

You may use brainstorming to generate measurement, reward, and reminder ideas. It's useful any time you are trying to generate creative approaches.

OBJECTIVE AND HABIT DEFINITION

Assuming the team has selected a specific habit they wish to develop, they now need to design the habit and its development and execution.

First, make sure everyone is clear on the overall objective, and why it is important.

The habit action should be clearly defined. Everyone on the team needs to have a thorough understanding of how it will work. The definition should answer these questions:
- What is the cue that triggers the habit?
- What exact habit action is expected of the team member?
- What are the exceptions so they don't take it too far?

Let's look at an example.

Assume the broad objective you challenged the team to solve was to increase the speed of service at checkout because it is a key factor for customers when they make a decision where to shop and more customers means more opportunities for team members to be able to work all the hours they want to work and make money. You have reviewed the process map with your team. They recognize that one of the factors that increases the customer's perception of a slow line is when a customer happens to select a register line in which the customer in front of them has a longer than normal checkout time due to a problem or a complex purchase. This can be very frustrating for the waiting customer and make them feel the line is longer than it really is.

The team reasons that a single line feeding all registers would eliminate this issue (because the next person in line gets to checkout next, not the customer who happened to have picked the "right" register). The team researches this idea and finds that stores that adopt the single line system do, in fact, reduce checkout time, beyond improving perceptions.

The team proposes that the store go to a one line set-up, which will require a new set of habits for team members. The team agrees that the most critical one is to get the customer to approach the open register as soon as possible so customers don't delay the main line. The store sets up a system of "available" lights for each register that the cashier turns on and off as appropriate. The new habit that must be developed is to get the cashiers to turn on and off the light at the most optimal time.

The team determines that the best time to turn the light on is when the current customer's receipt is printing. The light should be turned off the moment the next customer arrives at the register.

The habit is simple: flipping a switch either up or down. The next step is for the team to develop the cue that triggers the habit. In this example, the cue is obvious: when the payment goes through and the receipt starts printing, the cashier will flip the switch. The cue to turn it off is when the next customer reaches the register. The team may even consider adding a simple piggyback habit of the cashier speaking a customer welcome phase like, "Good afternoon," as they flip the switch off.

To build consistency, this habit should be implemented every time, even when the store is slow and the cashiers feel it may not be needed. The reality is that they do need to flip the switch in slow times so they may quickly build a consistent habit.

In this particular example, there are no exceptions. In the few cases when the habit action doesn't really need to be done, there is no downside if it is, and it helps quickly build this into an automatic habit.

As you plan other habits, you should consider whether the habit may be detrimental to the customer experience in some circumstances. For example, you may be developing a habit of asking a customer if they'd like to take advantage of a buy-one-get-one-free candy bar promotion when they check out at your store. Picture a customer holding a screaming baby who is buying milk for her baby. Think about her emotional state and whether you telling her about the promotion would make her experience better or more frustrating. In a situation like this, you would suspend the habit because she obviously only needs to buy the milk and give it to her baby.

If your quick service restaurant has a rewards program and you have a habit of telling each customer what rewards they are entitled to, don't do this with the customer who orders and finishes with, "I'm not going to use any rewards today."   He is likely saying it because he is aware of the rewards, is in a hurry, and does not want to hear them again. It would be detrimental to his experience if you listed off his rewards to him.

Use common sense when applying habits.   But don't allow a phony reason to get a team member out of being held accountable for performing the habit action.

TRACKING PERFORMANCE

How might the team track performance improvement?   There are several options:
- Managers could take turns monitoring the specific habit action and how well it is being followed using a tick sheet. Each cashier is tracked.   If they follow the habit as designed (flipping the "available" light switch when the current customer's receipt begins printing) the cashier gets a tick mark on the sheet.   They also get a tick mark every time they turn off the "available" light when the next customer approaches the register. This approach would not be a good long-term measure because it requires too much of the managers' time, but early on it might be a good way to get the habit established.
- If there is a video camera capturing the action at the registers, viewing the video in fast forward mode may allow for quicker tracking without taking as much of the managers' time.
- Another approach to monitoring and tracking this is to have team members keep track of successful habit action completion. They monitor other team members and mark the tick sheet. This provides the added benefit of bringing their full attention to the habit they should also be doing. Even having each cashier stand back and monitor the others for an hour would likely go a long way to helping the observing cashier develop the new habit.
- You could have the cashiers do a self-evaluation at the end of the day. They may grade themselves on how consistent they

were in following the new habit.   If they felt they did it every time, they would give themselves an A. They'd rate themselves a B for a few misses, and a C for more. If they struggled with it they might self-rate a D.   If they barely did it at all, they earned an F. Over several days they could compare their own daily grades to see if they are improving. By self-rating, the cashiers will likely be more focused on consistently performing the task.

- Team members who are following the new habit consistently should, over time, have higher transactions per hour than they had before the change. Obviously, some shoppers take more time to check out than others. However, over time, these shoppers should be distributed pretty evenly among the cashiers.   Looking at a few weeks of data should make for a fair comparison.   The advantage to this measure is that it really tracks the broader objective of checking out customers quicker, not just the habit action of turning the "available" light on and off.

- You could take a similar approach and make it a team measurement. Has the store increased average transactions per hour?

- You could measure wait time for customers.   At different times of the day a manager or team member at the line entrance hands a wait time card to a customer when they get in line. The simple index card has the current time written on it from a digital clock that is also visible to the cashiers. When the customer's transaction is complete, the customer hands the wait time card to the cashier who notes the time.   These are collected at the end of the day and the amount of wait time through transaction time is calculated.   The goal would be to reduce this over time.

- A broader measure is to understand how the new habit action has impacted customer perceptions. If you conduct a survey before you implement the new habit you could ask about satisfaction with the amount of time for the check out.   You might even ask customers to estimate how long it took from the time they got in line to the time they left.   While you may know this factually by using the wait time card method mentioned previously, the customers' perception is really more important than actual wait time because that perception will drive their future behavior. Repeat the survey after you've implemented the change, asking the same exact questions in the same way. If you are achieving your objective, it should be reflected in the results. When reviewing results, make sure you take into account any change in volume in your pre/post periods.

- It is also a good idea to get qualitative feedback regarding the changes you've made. If a manager knows some store "regulars" she might strike up a conversation with them and find out if they like the new system and the reasons why they do or don't. This feedback would be very helpful if there is a need to make an adjustment. Customer opinions might provide the team with additional improvement ideas. When the manager talks with customers, she needs to remember that opinions will vary. Some customers will naturally be resistant to any change. Others may be open to change but are disappointed they can no longer select the line of their "favorite cashier". All this should be considered and taken into account when considering customer feedback.

GOALS AND GOAL MILESTONES

Before you establish rewards, you need to determine an ultimate goal and your first milestone goal.

In our example you might think the best goal would be a certain level of positive ratings from customers on a survey. But is that really your objective? Your real objective is to provide your customers with a better experience so they will shop with you more and recommend your store more to friends. Your real objective is to increase sales.

If surveys are part of your measurement system, you may be tempted to focus on improved survey results as your daily goal. Often this is unwise. Survey results have a place, but only as a broader, long-term measure. If you are developing the right habits, and if you are practicing those habits consistently, you should expect higher ratings. If survey ratings don't improve over time, and you are certain that you are consistently practicing the habit, then you need to consider the possibility that the habit is not the right action to focus on, or that you have other habits you need to develop before you can achieve your goal.   In other words, your performance may be great, but it may not be the right action needed to achieve your goal.

The survey results are an indicator that you are on the right track, but because they are not totally impacted by you, you cannot totally control this outcome.

In addition, a focused daily goal of an improved rating on a survey could lead to temptations to "game" the survey.   Gaming is when someone tries to get higher ratings on surveys in ways other than improving the customer experience.   You've likely been to businesses engaged in this. They ask you to take a survey and rate them high. Sometimes they will say any rating lower than topbox is failure or that the security of their job is based on those survey results.   All these practices are very detrimental to the business because it makes the survey results unreliable. The business is flying blind. Worse, they think they are providing better customer service than they really are. These businesses sometimes publicize their high ratings in advertising. This is very misleading and unethical.

What individuals can control is the habit actions that they believe will lead to a better experience for customers. Your best, focused goals should be on consistent completion of the habit action.

Your team should have an ultimate goal. This is the level of performance that, if maintained consistently over time, would achieve your objective.   In our example, your ultimate goal might be that 95% of the time team members are turning the "available" light on and off based on the cues you've established.

Jumping to the ultimate goal is usually too difficult to do in one step. That's why it is wise to develop milestone goals. These are easier goals that progressively get more and more difficult, and lead you to your ultimate goal.

The milestone goal should be challenging but still very obtainable. There are a couple of ways to do this. One is to take the team average at a point in time and set a goal that everyone should achieve at least that level of performance. If your measure is an observation of how frequently team members perform the habit action after each cue, you might set a percent goal. After a week, calculate a team average and make that the individual goal for the following week.

Alternatively, the top quartile is a good target. With the top quartile you can point out that a quarter of the team has achieved that or better so it is in the realm of possibility for anyone on the team. If most team members are performing at a similar level, the top quartile is the best goal. If there are several struggling team members at much lower levels, you may consider a goal of achieving the team average. Your goals should be seen as achievable and possible for all or nearly all team members. If they are seen as unachievable, some may give up and you won't be as successful with your habit development plan.

Finally, you may set step level milestone goals based on different levels of performance. For example, you may plan to get to 100% habit action completion every time there is a cue. The first week it may be more realistic to set the milestone goal at 70% then 80% the following week, and 90% the week after that. It's good to have a general plan for your milestone goals up front, but to also be flexible to change based on team performance. If your first milestone goal is 70%, for example, and the team struggled just to get to 40%, you may need to adjust and set a goal of 50% or something else more attainable. Remember, we want to build momentum toward the goal without making it so challenging that team members don't believe it is possible.

REWARDS FOR INDIVIDUALS AND WORK TEAMS

What kind of rewards should the team select?

Rewards may be individual or team based. The advantage to individual based rewards is that individual team members feel that they have more control over the outcome. Because they know their performance alone will determine whether or not they are successful, each person is motivated to do a great job.

Team awards motivate the team as a whole to contribute. This could prompt positive peer pressure among team members for everyone to do well. In addition, an individual not motivated by an individual reward may not want to let the team down and may be motivated to improve performance.

Which is best? The answer is both. Designing individual and team rewards provides the best of both worlds. Individual effort is never wasted if people have control over successful performance. Team rewards lead to team work and a supportive environment.

The example measures suggested earlier could all lead to the intrinsic reward of pride—pride as an individual doing well, and pride as part of a team in which every member does well. To ignite this pride, measurement results have to be frequent and very visible.

To facilitate the intrinsic reward of pride, there must be constant performance visibility. For every measure(s) the team chooses, the results should be posted so everyone can see them. This may be as simple as writing results on a dry erase board in the break area or even posting results on a web page accessible by all team members. Set an initial habit-action consistency goal that each individual is expected to reach, and list the names of the team members who achieve it.

You will also want to show how well the team is doing. Post the team average daily or weekly. From time to time, as the team progresses, raise the goal. You may take the top quartile of the current time period as your new team goal for the next period.   This will help push everyone higher.

It's a good idea to track team progress over time. In this example, you might post a graph of the average each day or week.

Beyond visible displays of these measures, team progress should be discussed at every team meeting and when team members check in or out for their shift. This level of emphasis will allow the team members, individually and collectively, to enjoy the reward of intrinsic pride.

You may want to develop positive extrinsic rewards as well. This may also be individual or team based. There are many options. Top quartile or top team members may receive an extra break the next day they work, a small value gift card (e.g. for Starbucks, iTunes or Amazon), or some small merchandise item. The team may be rewarded with a team pizza party or a "Congratulations" cookie cake when various milestones are reached. In the appendix you will find a long list of suggested extrinsic rewards.

Let your work team develop rewards they think would be most motivating to the team, with your guidance of course. You may give them a list of various choices that you can support, such as extra breaks and the ability to select schedules. For rewards that cost money, provide a budget.

One creative approach is to "pay" team members and the entire team in made up play money (paper or virtual) that can be used in an auction of items at a later date. This way, rewards may be given frequently leading up to an auction of merchandise, movie tickets, days off, and a free car wash by the team manager. The list of possibilities may be endless. Then "money" is rewarded generously along the way, motivating daily, with the one payout at auction time.

Avoidance of negative intrinsic consequences may come for team members who need help because of their level of performance. These would be team members below a certain minimum goal. For example, if the team goal is 80%, the minimum may be 60%. Any team members under 60% might expect the manager to spend some time each day coaching them to do better. If you take this approach, you should set the minimum at what should be a very easily achievable goal.

Avoidance of negative extrinsic consequences may be that team members who do not achieve the minimum level cannot enjoy the team reward, or lose the option to sign up to work paid overtime when it is available.

ACTING ON PERFORMANCE MEASUREMENT RESULTS

If the team is consistently practicing the new habit and if customers perceive that the wait time has improved then the new habit is working well as designed.   If not, however, an adjustment or additional focus may be needed.

A couple of types of opportunities for improving may come out of your measures.   You may discover that the habit action is not being followed consistently, or you may discover that it is being followed but not accomplishing the broader objective of reducing perceived check out time from the customers' perspective.

If your measures show that team members are not consistently performing the new habit action of turning on and off the "available" light, you need to determine how to be more consistent.

First figure out if the entire team is struggling to adopt the new habit or if it is just a few individuals.
- If it is the entire team, you want to meet with the team and get feedback as to why they think adopting the new habit is so challenging. In this case, there appears to be a design flaw in your habit action implementation. Determine whether they are following the process as planned. If they are following it, find out why it's not working. This should come to light pretty quickly. If they are not following the habit action development process, find out what might be done so it is followed more consistently. Ask what the barriers are.
- If several members of the team are adopting the habit successfully, but others are not, you may have a similar conversation with the individuals who are struggling.   Also talk with team members who are successfully implementing the

new habit so they may shed light on things they are doing or thinking about differently that may be adopted by the struggling team members. The managers may have to direct their attention toward the struggling team members for a few days to help them adopt the habit successfully.

If your team is consistently practicing the habit, yet your measures do not show an improvement in overall wait time or perceptions of wait time, you will want to reexamine your system. Is the new habit creating unintended issues that are working against you? This is where what you learned from your conversations with customers would be extremely helpful in figuring out how your design might be altered.

REPLACING BAD HABITS

Since this habit does not replace any bad habits, or does not involve overcoming any bad habits, there is no need to develop a habit replacement process.

HABIT ACTION CONTINGENCY PLANS

The team should brainstorm barriers to habits and develop a contingency plan for each barrier.

What are some potential barriers to the habit action of flipping an "available" light on and off?
- The lightbulb may be burned out.
- The switch may not work.
- The store may be so slow that there isn't a line.
- When the receipt prints and the light goes on, the departing customer may ask a question about something on the receipt (e.g., they feel a price is incorrect).
- The next customer in line does not see the light come on.

Let's come up with a contingency plan for each of these.

If the lightbulb is burned out, it should be changed immediately. This means that new lightbulbs should be stored very close to the register areas, as well as any tools needed to change them (e.g., screwdriver to remove the cover, a step ladder, etc.). Several team members should be familiar with how to change the bulb.

If the switch isn't working, a replacement part should be readily available, as well as tools and clear instructions on how to replace it. If there is an unused register at the time, the cashier may move to that register while his register's "available" light switch is being repaired.

If there are very few customers in the store and there is no line, the action habit of turning the light on and off is not impacted.

If a departing customer needs to talk with the cashier after the "available" light has been activated, the cashier needs to decide quickly if this will be a brief or extended delay for the next customer. If brief, the cashier should greet the customer walking up and say he'll help the customer in just a moment. After taking care of the previous customer, the cashier should apologize for the delay. If the departing customer will be taking a longer period of time, the cashier should apologize to the approaching customer and ask them to wait for the next light.

If the next customer in line does not see the light, the cashier or another team member should politely ask the customer to approach the register. If there is a long bank of registers, the store may consider adding a more sophisticated system that verbally tells the next customer which register number to approach.

There is a possibility that the team does not think of all possible issues that may arise. Through experience, these will become evident. The team member will handle it as best she can in the moment, but the issue should be noted so that a standard contingency plan may be developed.

REMINDERS

The work team planning the new habit should determine reminders to keep the new habit top of mind.

We've already covered tracking and making this visible. This is a natural reminder that should be greatly leveraged.

The team could create index cards that could sit on or near the register. They could be straight forward and just state the cue and habit action.

> When the receipt prints, turn on the available light.
> When the next customer approaches, turn it off.

The team may also come up with alternate cards so that they change from time to time and keep attention. Here's an example:

> Paper up, light on.
> Customer up, light off.

Or

> Hear the printer, flip the switch up.
> Hear the next customer, flip the switch down.

These and other differently worded cards will keep the reminders fresh. The cards might also reference the current goal.

There may be other visible reminders. Examples include a poster in the break area, a label that says "light" on the cashier's side of the printer, or a hand signal the manager gives to remind cashiers who are forgetting the habit action.

ACCOUNTABILITY PARTNERS

Willpower is like a muscle that strengths through use, but also can get tired and fail. Like exercising a muscle, when you first begin practicing a habit your willpower is strong. However, over time, it will become weaker and you'll be tempted to be less consistent with the habit action.

That's where an accountability partner comes in. Think of an accountability partner as someone who steps in to help when your willpower is strained. Habit development is most successful when team members have an accountability partner to keep them on track.

They help in a couple of ways. They remind you to stay on track verbally and through example. At the same time, they leverage your pride. It's one thing to fail when no one else knows about it, but not to follow through on a commitment to a habit development plan when you are accountable to a peer who has made the same commitment is something altogether different.

While your entire work team is an accountability partner to each other, which is the basis of team habit development, you can leverage the importance of accountability in a second way. Each team member should be assigned one or two accountability partners. Their job is to work with each other and provide encouragement when someone's willpower needs a boost.   They do this through reminders and by setting a good example for each other.

The work team planning the new habit should develop an accountability partner plan. The team members whose work schedules overlap the most may be assigned to teams of two or three. They help hold each other accountable by reminding each other when they forget to follow through on the habit action.   If they don't work closely together they may meet from time to time and talk about the challenges of following the habit development plan and possible solutions. They encourage each other to follow the plan.

You may wonder why setting up accountability partners is necessary if the team manager is coaching for performance. The reason is that the manager cannot be in all places at all times. Some team members will perform the habit when the manager is around, but not be as consistent when she isn't.   Since the accountability partners work together, they get to see each other's performance all day long. The accountability partner serves as a surrogate when the manager is not around.

Earlier we discussed the value of team rewards. You may consider leveraging this further by also having "accountability team" rewards for the two or three team members who are accountability partners. Another option is to make the reward for the accountability team an intrinsic one by posting results by accountability team. Now if a team member fails, he fails not only himself, but also his small accountability team. This will put pressure on some team members to be more committed to the habit development plan.

For this example habit development plan, we might pair our cashiers up into accountability teams. The accountability teams are told that their role is to help each other stay accountable to follow the habit development plan. This is a place where hand signals may be especially useful.

We may also consider providing a reward of an extra break for the accountability team if they reach the overall team milestone each week.

If there isn't an opportunity to set up this kind of accountability partnership, because shifts don't overlap very much, you would still set up accountability partners so team members can briefly meet from time to time to discuss progress and how each other may be more consistent.

ENVIRONMENTAL FACTORS

Now it is time to identify potential environmental factors. With this particular habit, there are not many.

Beyond the contingency plans to combat negative environmental factors, the team should discuss habit action enablers. These may be things that support the habit. In our example, the store would set up a queue so the customers are in one line.   A sign explaining the light system (e.g., "Proceed to the register with an Available light") might be considered.

The switches must be easy to use and consistent in operation (e.g., forward is on and back is off on all of them).

Consistent coaching by the management team and store trainers is important, especially early on.   Team members need to be reminded whenever they forget to follow the habit action. This coaching and interaction with management is part of the environment.

We've applied the habit principles to an example habit.   The team may now try to tackle one based on the habit they selected.   In the next chapter we'll review the Habit Development Worksheet, which incorporates everything we've covered here.

ULTIMATE OUTCOME – BELIEFS ARE ALTERED

The desired outcome of any habit development plan is consistent performance of the habit with very little, if any, conscious awareness. When your team has successfully implemented the habit, something maybe even more important will have occurred. Your team members will have an altered belief.   They will go from believing their old behavior was either acceptable or the best they could do to believing the new behavior is the norm and that they are capable of performing it consistently.

This is extremely important and very significant. Without the change in their belief system, the habit would never stick. Due to this change, the habit will likely continue to be exercised unless management fails to monitor and make corrections when it is missed.

CHAPTER SUMMARY

Your work team will plan the first habit.
- Begin by process mapping the customer experience and the process from the business's perspective.

Team brainstorming is a great tool used to generate ideas.
- Clearly define the objective of the brainstorming session.
- Begin with silent brainstorming on slips of paper.
- Start brainstorming as a group.
- Collect every idea, do not evaluate or judge any idea at this point.

After several ideas have been generated, move into the evaluation phase.
- Make a list of pros and cons for the top ideas.
- Focus the team first on making a list of all the reasons it is a good idea.
- Then ask the group to name reasons it might not work well or result in negative consequences.

Use brainstorming to develop the habit definition. This should include three components:
- Cue that triggers the habit.
- Habit action.
- Exceptions.

Develop performance tracking.
- Brainstorm ideas from simple to sophisticated.

Set goals and milestones.
- They should be linked directly to the action.
- Beware of unintended consequences of some goals.

Develop a rewards plan for the habit.
- These may be individual, accountability team, or full team based.
- Explore both intrinsic and extrinsic rewards.

Determine how to address team members who do not follow the habit development plan.

Develop a habit replacement process if the team is attempting to overcome a bad habit.

Develop Habit contingency plans to overcome barriers to habit development.
- Determine what must be set up so these contingency plans may be implemented, if necessary.

Create reminders of the habit.

Determine how accountability partners will be assigned.

Examine environmental factors.
- Make adjustments to the work environment to enhance habit development.

Focus on altering the team members' beliefs about the team and themselves.

COMPLETE YOUR FIRST HABIT DEVELOPMENT WORKSHEET •····

WE'VE COVERED THE BASICS of habit development and many of the factors to keep in mind. Now we are going to introduce you to the Habit Development Worksheet that will help guide your team though the steps of habit development in an effective, organized manner.

1) Objective: Clearly state the overall objective of what the habit is designed to accomplish and the reason why it is important to accomplish the objective.

2) Habit Definition: Specifically define the habit action and which cue triggers it.

3) How We Will Track Performance: List of performance measurements.

4) Goal: The SMART goal of the habit action.

5) Goal Milestones: The mini-goals that mark progress toward the goal.

6) Individual Rewards: The rewards for individual team members based on individual team member goal completion.

7) Team Rewards: The rewards for team members based on team goal completion.

8) Action to Be Taken Based on Substandard Performance: Steps taken to help lagging team members adopt the habit.

9) Bad Habits to Replace: A description of any bad habits the new habit may be replacing.

10) Habit Action Contingency Plans: A list of possible barriers to habit action adoption and the corresponding action and preparation to overcome these.

11) Reminders: Visual, audio, or other reminders of the habit.

12) Accountability Partners: A list of assigned groups of two or three team members who help each other follow the habit development plan.

13) Environmental Factors: Adjustments that may be made to the environment to enhance habit adoption. This may include the assignment of specific accountability partners for each team member.

A Word template of this worksheet may be downloaded from WorkTeamHabits.com, code 11302.

Some of these items may not apply to some of the habit development plans. For example, new habits will not always replace bad habits.   In a few instances it may make sense to have either team or team member rewards, but not both. Most of the other items should be covered with each new Habit Development Plan.

We've already covered one habit thoroughly in the prior chapter. The remainder of this chapter consists of examples. When you meet with your team, you may want to review some of these more relevant examples.   Better yet, for practice, give your team the scenario and have them develop the plan.   Then compare their plan to the sample plan in the book to provide additional pointers.   There is no perfect right answer. Your team's approach may be quite different than our examples, but still be just as realistic.

Be careful not to take on too much.   If you focus on developing more than one or two habits at a time, you run the real risk of not mastering any of them. You do not want your team to be a "jack of all trades, but master of none."   They need to master those habits that are most important, and these habits take time and focus to develop to the point of consistency.

Scenario #1:   Your team works in a quick service restaurant. The health inspector visits your restaurant and cites you for several cleaning violations. The counter surfaces in the serving area, as well as the tables in the dining room, are not being sufficiently cleaned.   Your area manager wants this fixed immediately and tells you she expects you to show much improvement by the time the health inspector returns in three weeks.   You quickly organize your team and together write a habit development plan.

SCENARIO #1 WORKSHEET:

1) Objective: Greatly improve the consistency and quality of cleaning surfaces in the restaurant so that you don't lose any points for this on the next inspection in three weeks.
   • This is important because customers deserve and want a clean restaurant. In addition, continued violations could lead to the closing of the restaurant and the loss of jobs.

2) Habit Definition: Various cues lead to the team member wiping down the counter or table.

- Whenever any counter team member arrives for their shift or returns from a break they take five minutes to wipe down the serving counter.
- Whenever any counter team member finishes their shift they take five minutes to wipe down the serving counter.
- Anytime there is a spill on the counter, the team member closest to it immediately wipes it up.
- Whenever any dining room team member arrives for his shift, he walks the dining room and thoroughly wipes down every empty table.
- Whenever any dining room team member leaves from her shift, she walks the dining room and thoroughly wipes down every empty table.
- Whenever a customer leaves a table in the dining room, a team member walks up to the table and sprays it with disinfectant and wipes it down.

3) How We Will Track Performance: Various measures will be used.

- A check sheet is developed for team members to mark after they complete each cleaning.
- The manager will set her phone to alert her at the top of every hour. At that time she will check the counter and dining room for cleanliness and assign a grade for this hour (A = extremely clean, with no sticky spots or crumbs anywhere, to F = not at all clean). Notes are made to explain any grade less than an A. The grade and notes are written on a sheet that is posted for everyone to see.
- The opening team members will inspect the dining room and counters when they first come in and give the closing team members a grade based on what they see. If the grade is less than an "A," they provide details regarding how the closing team could have done better.
- The final outcome measure will be passing the next sanitation inspection, with a higher score.

4) Goal: Straight As on both the manager and opening team member grades.

5) Goal Milestones: First week – average grade of C or better. Second week – average grade of B or better. Final week – straight As.

6) Individual Rewards:
   - Team members who check the sheet indicating they cleaned on cue every time during their shift and who are graded an A each hour during their shift by the manager earn an entry in a draw to win a paid day off. The draw takes place at the end of the three weeks.
   - Each time a team member achieves five entries, he or she receives a free meal.
   - Members of the team will experience an intrinsic reward every time they check the sheet that they did their cleaning.
   - Team members who do not clean the counter when they first come in or return from break are assigned additional cleaning responsibilities.

7) Team Rewards: The rewards for team members based on team goal completion.
   - Each time the team goes three days in a row of perfect As from the manager and opening team, everyone who worked during that time receives a free cookie or other small food item of their choice.
   - If the team successfully passes the next health inspection, the management team provides them with a pizza party.
   - The team will experience an intrinsic reward every time they earn an A and when they pass the inspection.

8) Action to Be Taken Based on Substandard Performance:
   - If a manager notices that a team member does not wipe off the counter when they first arrive or return from break, they assign additional cleaning responsibilities to that team member that day.

9) Bad Habits to Replace: The bad habit that will be replaced is the habit of spilling something on the counter and ignoring it. This is replaced by the habit of cleaning up after every spill. The team member will still meet the psychological need of belonging (behaving like other team members).

10) Habit Action Contingency Plans:
   - The restaurant is very busy when the team member first arrives: The team member still wipes down the counter in whichever area he is working.
   - Towels cannot be found: Store an "emergency supply" of towels for situations like this. Replenish it the next day.
   - The sanitation water needs to be refilled: Refill it. The team member assigned to clean the dining room is responsible for filling up the sanitation bottles every shift.
   - Customers sit at the table before the team member has a chance to clean it: Assuming they haven't received their food yet, the team member politely asks the customer if he can wipe down the table for them.

11) Reminders: Visual and/or audio reminders of the habit.
   - A small reminder sign is posted at the clock in/clock out location.
   - Tracking papers, showing team progress, as well as the last sanitation report are also posted in the clock in/clock out area.
   - The manager displays a hand signal as a reminder when she sees a spilled area that needs wiping up.
   - Working team members remind checking in or returning from break team members to wipe down the counters, if they forget.

12) Accountability Partners: Small, assigned groups of two or three team members who help each other follow the habit development plan.
   - Team members who usually work the same shift are partnered in groups of two to four and serve as accountability partners. They call out misses in a helpful way, and compliment each other when consistent cleaning is completed through the shift.

13) Environmental Factors: Adjustments that may be made to the environment to enhance habit adoption.
- A towel is placed in the area where every team member stands (e.g., next to each register, next to the printer that prints the order, etc.).
- Clean towels and sanitizer bottles are readily available close to work areas.

Scenario #2: Your team is responsible for training new store managers in a large company. They visit the company headquarters when they are first hired and spend three days learning about leadership and company policies. You conduct class evaluations at the end of each three day session. These evaluations reveal that these new managers in training are generally complimentary about the training but suggest that the team could be more organized so less time is wasted.   You and your facilitators meet and discuss this.   The team process maps the class preparation process. Together, you figure out what the organization challenges are that cause the class materials to not always be available and organized well.

SCENARIO #2 WORKSHEET:

1) Objective: Have all class materials neatly organized for every class every time so that class participants may maximize the time they have in class.
- This is important because the benefit the participants receive from the class is impacted greatly by the amount of time the facilitator is able to spend covering the material and how easy it is for participants to follow along.

2) Habit Definition: All class materials are available and organized prior to the beginning of the class. This is done the business day before the first class. The trigger is that a team member is scheduled time to do this.   In addition, the next day in class the facilitator will note if anything is missing. The cue for making this note is if they have to get a replacement item or find something that is not in the right place.

3) How We Will Track Performance:
   - The facilitator who prepares the class materials the day before checks off each item on the "materials needed" list and includes the number of each material needed.
   - Facilitators will keep a log and note any time they don't have enough materials or that they have trouble finding the materials they need. This is scored at the end of each class.
   - With consistent practice of this habit, the class participant surveys should no longer raise "unorganized" as an issue. Of course, surveys must be presented in a very objective manner and no reference to "how well the class was organized" should be made by any facilitator.

4) Goal: "100% Ready" – meaning the right number of materials that are needed are properly organized for every class, every time.

5) Goal Milestones: Measure misses with the first class and set a schedule to improve this with each successive class until the team is "100% Ready."

6) Individual Rewards:
   - The team member who prepares the material the night before is told how they did by the class facilitator the next day. The facilitator reviews their "materials needed" list and how well the preparing team member did. The preparing team member can take pride in consistent improvement.
   - The log of how well materials were prepared is posted so all team members may learn from it. This may be a source of recognition and pride for the preparing team members, based on their performance.
   - The manager of the facilitators provides each facilitator with feedback on whether they were observed consistently making note of missing materials. The facilitators may take pride in doing a good job of tracking improvement.

7) Team Rewards:

- When the facilitator check list shows five class sessions in a row are perfect, and at those same sessions comments about the class organization are not negative, then the team can add "100% Ready" to the list of how they describe themselves as a team.

8) Action to Be Taken Based on Substandard Performance:
- If the team member responsible for preparing materials consistently fails to include the correct materials, a "practice session" is set up with the team manager so the manager can help identify why the team member is missing items and what new procedures might help the team member do a better job.

9) Bad Habits to Replace:
- Replace the bad habit of rushing through material preparation and not making sure everything is prepared properly with the habit of following the "materials needed" list. They enjoy the psychological benefit of knowing they are doing what is expected of them.

10) Habit Action Contingency Plans:
- Materials not available for the material preparer: since he is preparing them the night before, he has time to make additional copies. To facilitate this, up-to-date electronic copies of all training materials should be available.
- The computer from which copies are printed is not working: either use another computer or make copies from a "master materials hard copies" folder.
- The copier breaks as the materials are being assembled: another copier in the building or even at a local copy center is identified as the "go-to" location if this happens.
- The stapler jams, or the preparing team member runs out of staples or paper clips or other items needed for material assembly: the preparing team member has a company credit card or a "petty cash" fund so he may go to a local store and purchase whatever is needed.
- The classroom is not available for set-up. The class preparer alerts the team manager and either the preparer, the facilitator,

or team leader arrives early the next morning to set up for the class.

11) Reminders:
- The preparing team member is specifically scheduled for this task.
- The performance log is posted in the set-up area.
- A "Goal: 100% Ready" sign is placed in the set-up area.

12) Accountability Partners:
- The preparing team members are assigned an accountability partner. They check in from time to time and discuss consistency, what the circumstances of misses and successes were, and what can be learned from both.

13) Environmental Factors:
- The set up area is neat and organized and well stocked.
- The checklist of items needed is clear and complete.
- Communication in regards to the number of class participants is consistent and accurate.

Scenario #3: You manage a gas station. Through talking with customers you find out that their biggest frustration is when they have to come inside to get a receipt because the pumps are often out of receipt paper. Although you've mentioned this to your team a few times, the situation hasn't improved. It's time to instill a team habit.

SCENARIO #3 WORKSHEET:

1) Objective: Improve the customer experience by always having receipt paper in the printers.
- This is important because your customers will be able to count on the fact that their experience at your gas station will be hassle-free. When your business is seen as dependable and consistent, you will gain more revenue and be able to offer more opportunities to your staff.

2) Habit Definition: Change the receipt paper whenever a pump reaches 500 transactions since the last paper change. Transaction counts are checked every hour on the hour.   The cue is the top of the hour.

3) How We Will Track Performance:
   * Each time the receipt paper is replenished, write down how many transactions happened since the last change.
   * Keep track of the number of times a customer has to come in and ask for a receipt because the printer is out.

4) Goal: Every customer gets a receipt at the pump for a full week. This goal continues each week.

5) Goal Milestones:
   * Week #1: Just two customers a day need a receipt from inside and 80% of the time the rolls are changed before they reach 525 transactions.
   * Week #2: Just one customer a day needs a receipt from inside and 90% of the time the rolls are changed before they reach 525 transactions.
   * Week #3: Only three customers a week need a receipt from inside and 95% of the time the rolls are changed before they reach 525 transactions.
   * Week #4: No customers need a receipt from inside for an entire week and 98% of the time the rolls are changed before they reach 525 transactions.

6) Individual Rewards:
   * The pride of not having any customers needing to come in for a receipt during the team member's shift because they replenished the receipt paper on time.
   * Free candy bar of choice to team members who don't have any misses during five shifts in a row.

7) Team Rewards:
   * Whenever the team achieves the weekly milestone, everyone on the team receives a free soda to celebrate the success.

8) Action to Be Taken Based on Substandard Performance:
   - If a pump runs out of receipt paper, a manager talks with the team members to write up a description of the miss: when it happened, why it happened, and what can be done in the future to prevent it from happening again.

9) Bad Habits to Replace: not applicable.

10) Habit Action Contingency Plans:
   - The store runs out of receipt paper: The manager who orders inventory needs to make sure there is plenty on hand, checking inventory once a week. It's also advisable to keep a reserve stash in a specific area.
   - A team member cannot get the receipt printer open to change the paper, or some other mechanical difficulty: team member knows who to call to get help. Also, all team members should be thoroughly trained on how to change the receipt paper.
   - Sometimes a roll doesn't last 500 transactions: lower the transaction number for changing the roll.
   - The team members are very busy helping customers: the second team member should quickly change the paper because running out of paper at the pump will only increase the line inside.

11) Reminders:
   - Put a clock in the counter area that makes a sound at the top of every hour to remind the team members to check the transaction counts for each pump.
   - If the register can be programmed, have a message pop up reminding the team member to check the count at the top of the hour.
   - Put a small sign where team members clock in that states the current goal and shows the measures toward it.

12) Accountability Partner:
   - Each team member is assigned an accountability partner. They check in from time to time and discuss consistency, what the

circumstances of misses and successes were, and what can be learned from both.

13) Environmental Factors:
- Paper roll storage is organized and easy to access.
- Clear process for disposing removed rolls of paper.
- Quick and easy way to determine transaction counts at the top of every hour for all the pumps.

Scenario #4: You work in an office and you meet with your team several times during the week. The meetings often start 10 to 15 minutes behind schedule because team members are late. This wastes time and does not allow you and your team to create as much value for your internal customers.

SCENARIO #4 WORKSHEET:

1) Objective: All team members who attend department meetings arrive on time.
- This is important because starting meetings on time shows respect for all team members and allows the team to accomplish more in the meeting, to the benefit of the team and its customers (internal and external).

2) Habit Definition: Arrive at the meeting on time or early. The cue is the meeting time and the Outlook reminder that alerts you five minutes before the meeting. Don't take this habit too far by arriving at the meeting early at the expense of not completing a very important conversation that is extremely time sensitive.

3) How We Will Track Performance: The meetings all begin on time. Anyone arriving late is noted.

4) Goal: All meetings begin on time with everyone attending present and ready to engage in the discussion.

5) Goal Milestones:
- First week, 70% of meeting attendees on time.

- Second week, 80% of meeting attendees on time.
- Third week, 90% of meeting attendees on time.
- Fourth week, all meeting attendees on time for every meeting.

6) Individual Rewards:
   - The pride of having a reputation of being on time.
   - Not having the manager meet with you about being prompter.

7) Team Rewards:
   - Pride among team members due to everyone being on time.
   - Team members feeling they are respected and valued by everyone on the team.

8) Action to Be Taken Based on Substandard Performance: Team members who have the worst record of being on time meet with the manager. These team members have shown a pattern of being late. The manager asks them what is causing them to be late. They also discuss how being late to meetings comes across as being disrespectful to the other team members who arrive on time. Together they figure out how to help the team member get to the meetings on time.

9) Bad Habits to Replace: Being late due to staying on their computer too long, or another meeting running over. The psychological benefit is of belonging (being like the other team members).

10) Habit Action Contingency Plans:
    - Previous meeting runs over: meetings should end five minutes before the top of the hour so team members may get to their next meeting. If a meeting facilitator cannot manage a meeting to end on time, they may need facilitation coaching. A participant in such a meeting should be encouraged to leave the meeting when it was supposed to end so she's not late to her next meeting.
    - A meeting participant is tied up and just cannot break away: he should send a text message to the meeting facilitator of the next meeting, explaining how late he will be and why.

11) Reminders:
- Small "On Time, Every Time" table top cards are in the meeting rooms and provided to team members.
- Meeting invitations sent via Outlook always have a 5 minute reminder included.
- At the beginning of each meeting the facilitator thanks the team for arriving on time.

12) Accountability Partner:
- Each team member is assigned an accountability partner. They check in from time to time and discuss how well they do in arriving to meetings on time, what the circumstances of misses and successes were, and what can be learned from both.

13) Environmental Factors:
- Clocks are installed in every meeting room – all synced together.
- Meetings are well organized with a clear agenda and objectives. Meetings get down to business quickly.
- Meetings end 5 minutes before the top of the hour so participants may get to their next meeting on time and so team members meeting in that conference room can arrive and be ready to begin at the top of the hour.

Scenario #5: You are responsible for a team of nurses in a hospital. You investigate why the incidents of infection are running higher at your hospital than the national average and determine that it could be due to nurses not always washing their hands before assisting patients. While everyone is aware of the importance of hand washing, you notice that many of your team members forget.

SCENARIO #5 WORKSHEET:

1) Objective: Reduce the incidence of infections in your hospital through more consistent hand washing by nurses.

- This is important because just one miss of a nurse washing his or her hands could lead to a serious infection in a patient, potentially leading to death.

2) Habit Definition: Whenever a nurse enters a patient's room they first wash their hands.

3) How We Will Track Performance:
    - Team leader observes and documents consistency. Each time the team leader sees a nurse walk into a patient's room, she writes down whether or not they wash their hands.
    - Self-reporting by nurses: Every shift as they check out, each nurse marks on their sheet their estimated level of consistency for that hour. Options: 5 = perfect, 4 = one miss, 3 = two misses, 2 = three misses or don't recall, 1 = did not wash their hands.

4) Goal: 100% of the nurses wash their hands 100% of the time by the fourth week.

5) Goal Milestones (percent of time washing hands):
    - Week #1: 50% of nurses are perfect, team at 80%.
    - Week #2: 75% of nurses are perfect, team at 90%.
    - Week #3: 90% of nurses are perfect, team at 95%.
    - Week #4: 100% of nurses are perfect, team at 100%.

6) Individual Rewards:
    - Nurses reaching 100% get their name on the "Keeping Our Patients Safe From Infections" board and take pride in knowing they are consistently taking an important step in keeping their patients safe.
    - Every nurse achieving 100% handwashing for five days in a row gets one extra break.
    - Any nurse who achieves 100% hand washing for four weeks straight earns a special pin they wear. They temporarily lose the pin for a week if they forget to wash their hands.

7) Team Rewards: The rewards for team members based on team goal completion.
   - Challenge another group of nurses to be the group with the best percent of hand washing. Results are posted in both areas. The winning team is proud of their accomplishment.
   - When the team reaches one week of 100% consistency, a team photograph is made and a copy provided to each member of the team.
   - When the team reaches 100% consistent hand washing for four weeks in a row, everyone on the team attends a dinner with the hospital president.

8) Action to Be Taken Based on Substandard Performance:
   - Team members who miss more than the team goal (e.g. wash their hands less than 80% the first week, 90% the second week, etc.) meet with the team leader to discuss what can be done to help them improve. After two such meetings, the team member receives a reprimand.

9) Bad Habits to Replace: Rushing through their duties in assisting patients so quickly that they forget to wash their hands. The psychological reward is an even better feeling of serving their patients well.

10) Habit Action Contingency Plans:
   - Out of soap: go wash hands in another sink and immediately report it to the custodial team so the soap may be replenished.
   - Out of paper towels: go wash hands in another sink and immediately report it to the custodial team so the paper towels may be replenished.
   - Water not working: go wash hands in another sink and immediately report it to the maintenance team so repairs may be made.

11) Reminders:
   - Kick off effort with a short session about the importance of washing hands and the impact that forgetting has on patients.

Tell and post stories of real people who developed infections in hospitals due to nurses forgetting to wash their hands.

- Develop a symbol that means "wash hands." Put this on small stickers and place them in various locations where nurses are sure to see them during the day (e.g., on equipment, clipboards, etc.).
- In the list of items that nurses review with their patients, have them talk about the importance of any visitor washing their hands and have the nurse make a commitment to the patient that he or she will always wash their hands before they interact with the patient.
- Consider installing a sensor in the door of every hospital room that "dings" whenever someone enters, reminding nurses to wash their hands.

12) Accountability Partner:
- Each team member is assigned an accountability partner. They check in from time to time and discuss consistency, what the circumstances of misses and successes were, and what can be learned from both.

13) Environmental Factors:
- Have the custodial team keep the soap dispensers full, refilling them as soon as they get to the half way mark.
- Have the custodial team keep the paper towel dispensers full. They should be restocked whenever they get to the one-third full mark.
- Provide back-up soap and paper towels at the nurses' station so these may be replenished if a sink runs out and a custodial team member isn't immediately available.
- Make sure tracking sheets are organized and easily accessible.
- Team leader needs to spend several hours per week monitoring team performance the first week, and less and less the following weeks as the team performance improves.

Scenario #6: You are manager of the front desk of a hotel. Your general manager did some research and reviewed the last three months of customer comments on Trip Advisor. One issue that quickly came to light is that guests were not aware of free Wi-Fi in the room. Even though information was left in each room, somehow the guests were missing it.   You have been asked to make sure your front desk team tells every guest checking in that Wi-Fi is available and to call the front desk if they have any challenges in getting it to work.

SCENARIO #6 WORKSHEET:

1) Objective: Clearly communicate to every guest that the hotel has Wi-Fi available for all guests.
   * This is important because it serves your guests well and leads to better feedback in Trip Advisor, making your hotel more appealing.

2) Habit Definition: Guests are told about the availability of Wi-Fi as the key card is handed to them.

3) How We Will Track Performance:
   * Percent of time each guest is told about the availability of Wi-Fi when they check in: there are two jars on the desk. At the beginning of the day one is filled with pennies. Each time a guest is told about Wi-Fi, a penny is removed from one jar and placed in the other jar. At the end of the night all the pennies are counted and compared to the number of parties who checked in that day.
   * The number of complaints on Trip Advisor about Wi-Fi not being available. This is reviewed each week and posted by the manager.
   * Add a question to the hotel survey asking guests if they were aware that Wi-Fi was available.

4) Goal:
   * 100% of guests are told about Wi-Fi and no guests complain on Trip Advisor about not knowing about it for an entire month.

5) Goal Milestones:
   * Week #1: 70% of guests are told about Wi-Fi.

- Week #2: 80% of guests are told about Wi-Fi.
- Week #3: 90% of guests are told about Wi-Fi.
- Week #4-7: 100% of guests are told about Wi-Fi.

6) Individual Rewards:
- Each day that the front desk team members tell every guest about Wi-Fi they get entered into a weekly draw. If some team members work much shorter shifts than others, the team members get one entry per hour worked. The weekly winner receives a Starbucks, Target, or Walmart $25 gift card.

7) Team Rewards:
- Team member takes pride in achieving milestone goals.
- Special team dinner when the goal of 100% of guests told of Wi-Fi for four weeks is reached.

8) Action to Be Taken Based on Substandard Performance:
- If a manager notices a team member checking in a guest and forgetting to tell the guest about Wi-Fi, the manager meets with the team member and they discuss what can be done so that the front desk team member will remember to tell the guest.

9) Bad Habits to Replace: not applicable.

10) Habit Action Contingency Plans:
- The Wi-Fi is not working: team member still tells guests about Wi-Fi being available, but that it isn't working. Then they offer to call the guest when it is working again if they plan to use it.
- The guest does not speak English: Have cards available at the front desk in various languages that explain how to access Wi-Fi. The team member shows the appropriate card to the guest.

11) Reminders:
- "Tell Every Guest About Wi-Fi, Every Time" small note situated near check-in computer monitor.
- Post results of previous days and a list of past gift card winners on the team.

- Develop a hand signal that team members can use to remind each other.

12) Accountability Partner:
- Each team member is assigned an accountability partner. Ideally, these are team members who work the front desk together and are in positions to observe each other's work. They check in from time to time and discuss consistency, what the circumstances of misses and successes were, and what can be learned from both.

13) Environmental Factors:
- Keep the Wi-Fi network properly maintained and working with minimum downtime.
- Provide written Wi-Fi instructions that team members may offer to guests.

Scenario #7: You are the principal of an elementary school. Your school highly values parental involvement in the education of the students. The PTA recently implemented a key initiative to help facilitate greater parent support. A website has been developed that allows parents to see the progress their children are making in various subjects. For this to work, however, teachers need to regularly post grades and notes. The more consistently they do this the more involved parents are in helping ensure students do their homework, and supporting the teacher in addressing potential problems before they get out of hand. The issue is that the teachers seem to have challenges in getting into the habit of posting to the website, a task that takes less than 20 minutes per day.

SCENARIO #7 WORKSHEET:

1) Objective: Post accurate, timely information about student progress and how parents may assist in the education of their children. In some cases, this will lead to a quick conversation between parent and child to recap and reinforce what they learned that day. Ultimately, the students benefit as well as teachers

because teachers partner with parents in educating the students. Eventually, this should be reflected in the school's performance.

- This is important because the more parents partner with teachers in educating their children the more successful their children will be in school and later in life.

2) Habit Definition: Within an hour after the conclusion of each school day, the teacher posts some useful information about the progress of each student. This is usually in the form of topics covered, homework assigned, grades earned, and additional help that the student may need. Occasionally the teacher may mention additional issues like minor disciplinary concerns.   More significant concerns are discussed directly between the parents and teachers.

3) How We Will Track Performance: Track completion of daily posts for all students and review the quality of the posts. Completion of daily posts is tracked by the computer program. Quality is spot checked by the principal. The principal should spend several hours checking the first week and fewer and fewer hours in successive weeks, assuming the quality level is high.

4) Goal: At the end of each school day, post the progress of each student and explain how the parent may help.

5) Goal Milestones:
- Week #1: one post for each student at the conclusion of the week.
- Week #2: at least two posts per student per week.
- Week #3: at least three posts per student per week.
- Week #4: at least four posts per student per week.
- Week #5: five posts per student per week.

6) Individual Rewards:
- Progress is posted in the teacher's personal record and referenced in their end of year evaluation.
- "Teacher-Parent Partnership Hall of Fame" page on website lists names of teachers who achieve or exceed the goal milestone

and the parents who consistently review the site to monitor their child's performance.
- Teachers who achieve the milestone have their name entered into a weekly draw the first five weeks. The winner receives an afternoon off work as the principal covers their class for them.

7) Team Rewards:
- When the entire school is consistent in posting daily progress for four weeks in a row, a press release is prepared and distributed that is very complimentary of teacher and parent efforts in using the new tool to help their students do better.

8) Action to Be Taken Based on Substandard Performance:
- Teachers who do not meet the goal milestones need to meet with the principal to explain why they were not able to and to develop a plan to get on track the following week.

9) Bad Habits to Replace: not applicable.

10) Habit Action Contingency Plans:
- Can't log on to site or Wi-Fi at school is not working: Alert the principal who will arrange to have the problem fixed. Teachers may try at home if they have access.
- No grades to report, no homework assigned, and no requests of parents: post short note about what was covered in class that day. Parents may still be encouraged to ask their child about what they learned and see if they have any questions about it.
- Parents aren't logging in or don't seem to be involved: The teacher contacts the parents to find out why.   If the parent doesn't have internet access, the teacher prints out his or her notes and sends them home with the child.

11) Reminders:
- Since the trigger is the end of the school day (usually at the conclusion of the last class), a small table top card that says "3pm: Report to Parents" would be useful.
- The principal could make a brief, encouraging announcement on the PA system a couple of minutes after the last class ends,

thanking the teachers and reinforcing the importance of this habit.
* Post a copy of the latest "Teacher-Parent Partnership Hall of Fame" page on the wall of the teacher lounge.

12) Accountability Partner:
* Each teacher is assigned an accountability partner. They check each other's page each evening to see if progress about each student was posted and send a reminder to the other if it wasn't. In addition, they check in from time to time and discuss consistency, what the circumstances of misses and successes were, and what can be learned from both.

13) Environmental Factors:
* This program is rolled out to parents and teachers with a great deal of excitement, stressing the importance of parental involvement. The more parents use the information the easier it will be to get the teachers to post status updates.
* Teachers and parents are fully trained to use this website. Additional training modules are available on YouTube so they may be consulted in the future as needed.
* Wi-Fi at the school and teacher computers are well maintained.
* The principal mentions the program, the importance, and progress at every meeting with teachers and parents.

Scenario #8: You manage a delivery service. While your company rarely loses a package, on many occasions packages are not properly tracked through the process, causing concern for customers. You quickly recognized that accurate and consistent scanning of items through the delivery process is important to your customers and often impacts on whether they will use your service in the future.

SCENARIO #8 WORKSHEET:

1) Objective: Scan every package, at every transition point, every time.

- This is important because accurate scanning lets customers know that their important package is being monitored throughout the process. This is a critical factor that customers value when selecting a delivery service.

2) Habit Definition: Scan a package every time it is handled. The cue is touching the package.

3) How We Will Track Performance: Track the percent of packages in the system that are tracked correctly from start to finish.

4) Goal: Achieve 99.9% accurate tracking within 8 weeks.

5) Goal Milestones:

- Week #1: 80% accurate tracking.
- Week #2: 85% accurate tracking.
- Week #3: 90% accurate tracking.
- Week #4: 95% accurate tracking.
- Week #5: 98% accurate tracking.
- Week #6: 99% accurate tracking.
- Week #7: 99.5% accurate tracking.
- Week #8: 99.9% accurate tracking.

6) Individual Rewards:

- Team members feel pride in having their name on the "Scanning Accuracy" posted list when they achieve the milestone goal of accurate tracking, with their tracking accuracy percent.

- Team members who achieve the goal milestone of accurate tracking for the week earn an extra break that week.

- Team members who achieve 100% accurate tracking for the day receive an entry into the weekly draw for a $100 visa card.

7) Team Rewards:

- Each team member receives a team shirt when the goal of 99.9% accurate tracking is reached.

- Each month thereafter that the team achieves 99.9% tracking, each team member receives a $25 bonus.

8) Action to Be Taken Based on Substandard Performance:

- If a team member averages below the team milestone, they will meet with the manager to discuss how they can meet the goal the following week.

9) Bad Habits to Replace: not applicable.

10) Habit Action Contingency Plans:

- Scanning equipment not working: get it repaired as quickly as possible, go to alternate scanning method (if there is one), and don't count this downtime period in accurate scanning statistics.

- Label is damaged and can't be scanned: replace the label so scanning and tracking is possible. This requires system and supplies so it may easily be done.

11) Reminders:

- "Every Package, Every Time" signs in scanning areas.

- Additional signs with humorous/serious quotes about scanning and tracking. These signs change each week.

- Customer compliments about great tracking are shared with team members in team meetings.

- Post a sticker with a scanning symbol to the dashboard of each of the delivery trucks.

- A reminder is printed on their paycheck each week.

12) Accountability Partner:

- Each team member is assigned an accountability partner. They check in from time to time and discuss consistency, what the circumstances of misses and successes were, and what can be learned from both.

13) Environmental Factors:

- Make sure all scanning equipment is properly maintained and always working.

- The systems are arranged so that the scanning stickers are easy to identify and scan.

- The scanners provide an audio signal that the scan went through successfully.

NOW IT IS YOUR TEAM'S TURN

After thoroughly reviewing some of these examples of the 13 steps, your team should be well prepared to develop a plan for your work team's objective. Just talk through each step in order and decide what you will do. Don't worry if it is not perfect. Think of your plan as flexible and adjust it as you go, applying what you and your team learn along the way.

CHAPTER SUMMARY

The Habit Development Worksheet includes these 13 elements:

1) Objective: Clearly state the overall objective of what the habit is designed to accomplish and the reason why it is important to accomplish the objective.

2) Habit Definition: Specifically define the habit action and which cue triggers it.

3) How We Will Track Performance: List of performance measurements.

4) Goal: The SMART goal of the habit action.

5) Goal Milestones: The mini-goals that mark progress toward the goal.

6) Individual Rewards: The rewards for individual team members based on individual team member goal completion.

7) Team Rewards: The rewards for team members based on team goal completion.

8) Action to Be Taken Based on Substandard Performance: Steps taken to help lagging team members adopt the habit.

9) Bad Habits to Replace: A description of any bad habits the new habit may be replacing.

10) Habit Action Contingency Plans: A list of possible barriers to habit action adoption and the corresponding action and preparation to overcome these.

11) Reminders: Visual, audio, or other reminders of the habit.

12) Accountability Partners: A list of small, assigned groups of two or three team members who help each other follow the habit development plan.

13) Environmental Factors: Adjustments that may be made to the environment to enhance habit adoption. This may include the assignment of specific accountability partners for each team member.

PREPARE TO PUT THE HABIT DEVELOPMENT PLAN INTO ACTION •····

AT THIS POINT, your team has developed a Habit Development Plan and filled out the worksheet in all 13 areas. Congratulations! You've accomplished a big step. It's now time to set the team up for success.

Before your meeting is over, you will want to assign responsibilities and timelines to members of the team so you will execute your plan successfully. In addition, having these simple responsibilities to support habit development will get team members even more invested in the habit development and likely more supportive of it. To fully leverage this benefit, you should try to assign some preparation tasks to each member of the team.

If there is a broader team that was not involved in the habit development planning, you will need to communicate the plan to them in a compelling manner to gain both understanding and buy-in. This may be done by the team leader or by members of the planning team.

Look over your plan and determine which parts need some additional work. Assign these items to team members for follow-up. Provide whatever tools and resources they need and make sure they have a clear deadline. These may include such things as:

- Determine who will be measuring progress toward the goal, how this will done, and how and when regular results will be reported.
- Someone needs to purchase or create the rewards that are to be used for motivation, for both individuals and the team. These need to be prepared so they may be presented promptly, as soon as they are earned.
- Usually, the manager or team leader will be responsible for taking action with team members if they are not preforming at the expected level. This needs to be planned so that timely action is taken.
- Contingency plans must be reviewed for additional required preparation. These various activities may be assigned to several members of the team. It's a good idea to have all contingency plan materials in place before launching the habit development, but you don't want this to delay launch of habit development if a contingency is highly unlikely to be needed.
- Reminders, both audio and visual, need to be created. Some, like rotating signs, may not be used for a few weeks but they should all be developed and ready to go up front.
- Environmental adjustments should be taken care of within an assigned timeframe.

Let's go into a little more detail for each of these.

COMMUNICATING THE PLAN AND GAINING BUY-IN

If the team members who planned the habit development were a portion of the team, you need to develop a communication plan so that everyone on the broader team is aware of the plan, why it is important, and how it will impact them.

All members of the broader team should first go through the information provided in Chapter 3: Providing Team Members with Habit Development Knowledge.   Your team members will need to have this knowledge to fully appreciate the plan you and the other team members have developed, and how the plan will work. It allows the team to talk about habit development in the same way.   This investment of time is well worth the effort.

With this baseline understanding, it should be a relatively easy task to hand out copies of the habit development plan and review it with team members.   If the team size is manageable, it may be a good idea to allow discussion and some minor tweaking of the plan. This will lead to more buy-in from the broader team.

THREE TYPES OF TEAM MEMBERS

In these meetings you will likely have three types of team members:
1) Fully Supportive: These team members understand the importance and process of habit building. They understand the importance of the objective the team is focusing on, and they are committed to being good team players and fully engaging in the plan.
2) On-The-Fence: These team members are a little hesitant. This may be based on one of several reasons:
   • They do not fully understand the nature of habits and how creating habits will actually make their jobs easier and allow them to create more value for their customers.
   • They do not fully understand or agree with the process of habit development. They may not feel that focusing on a new habit for several weeks is necessary to make that habit become a part of the culture. Or they may not appreciate the importance of consistency and feel that a miss here or there is not a big deal.

- They may not see the importance of the team's habit development objective. They may not see what's in it for them and for the future success of the business.
- They may not be impressed with the reward ideas the team has developed and feel they would not be motivating enough.
3) Resistant: These team members are negative toward the habit development plan. They may state their objections verbally to the group or one on one with other members of the team. They will justify their feelings, usually based on spurious excuses, but in their mind these reasons to resist the plan are legitimate.

Management should express appreciation to those fully supportive team members. The habit development would not be possible without their support.

On-the-fence team members need to see the strong buy-in from "fully supportive" team members. These team members may be able to convince the "on-the-fence" team members to fully participate in the plan. It's also a good idea for managers to meet individually with team members they believe may be "on-the-fence". Their initial goal in these meetings is not to lecture the team member about habit development, but to understand why they are hesitant to support the plan. They can do this by discussing the points above.
- Ask them questions about the nature of habits.
  - What habits do they use every day?
  - How do those habits benefit them?
  - What would it be like if they had to consciously think through every step they take in every action they perform?
  - Do they recognize how much easier and less stressful it is to drive a car now than the first day they learned?
  - Would they like their job to be easier so they automatically do what's important without having to put much thought into it?
  - Would they like to add value for their customers by consistently carrying out a task that customers have identified as being very important?

- Ask them about habit development.
    - How long do they think it takes to develop a habit? If they answer with a very short period of time, ask for what reasons they think habits can be developed that quickly.
    - What habits have they personally developed in the past that quickly?
    - Do they believe everyone on the team can be consistent with new habits in the same period of time?
    - Where do they shop as a customer from time to time that they think does an okay, but not great job? Does this place occasionally do a great job? Do they sometimes do a poor job? So is the real issue lack of consistency in doing a great job?
    - How can a person or team have a goal of 100% (or near 100%) consistency without being strict about following the new habit?

- Ask them about the team's habit-building objective.
    - Why do they believe this is not an important objective?
    - Do they understand how the team leadership came up with this objective? If not, share the research process with them.
    - What important objective should the team focus on instead? If appropriate, add it to a list of potential future habit development opportunities.
    - If they still think another objective is more important, would they at least agree to support it as part of a "practice habit" for the team to learn the habit development process before moving on to more challenging habits?

- Ask them about the rewards.
    - Do they find the rewards motivating? Why or why not?
    - Do they feel the rewards are achievable? Why or why not? If possible, share some encouraging information so they may be more open to their chances of success.

The resistant team members are the most challenging. If you are not careful they can derail your entire effort. You will want to meet individually with these team members. To understand their point of view, you may first go through the questions you would use with the on-the-fence team members.

These team members may object to the habit development plan because they do not fully understand the different aspects of the value of habits, habit development, and why the selected objective is so important to the future success of their role and the company. You may be able to get them to see that the plan is more important or more likely to succeed than they first thought. If so, get them to agree to participate and support the team in the development of the habit.

Let them explain why they don't support the habit development initiative. Don't challenge their points in the moment but make a list of their concerns. Make sure they feel heard by asking clarifying questions and taking a lot of notes. Push them to really focus on facts and not opinions. The difference? Opinions may be challenged (e.g., "It's a beautiful day") while facts cannot be challenged (e.g., "It is 75 degrees outside with no clouds"). Acknowledge the facts they raise that are valid.

Usually, people disagree because they value or judge the same facts differently. Your job at this point is to understand differences in values or judgement regarding key facts. After they have expressed their concerns, say, "Thank you; is there anything else you'd like to bring up that we should consider?"

Now you have a decision to make. If they only raised a few facts and you feel prepared to present the team's point of view regarding them then proceed. If, however, you really need some time to think through the points raised, you can thank the team member for their thoughts and tell them you want to think them through and meet again the next day to discuss. This allows you to make notes and be prepared to attempt to change their perspective.

You may be wondering why you need to go through all this. You feel that you are the boss and they should just do what you tell them to do. While this is true, it is also short-term thinking. These team members may reluctantly go along with you, but if forced this way they will undermine the development plan and the team to the degree that you will have a very hard time stopping it. This is why it is important to persuade them to agree with the plan rather than force it on them.

If they are still resistant, they may have a deep-seated fear of change. You might talk to them about the importance of change. Point out that there have been large, very successful companies that went out of business because they did not adjust to the needs of their customers and failed to create greater value. Let them know that you will not allow your company to fail due to resisting necessary change. Too many team members depend on the success of the company to allow that to happen. Tell them you understand that change may be challenging and pushes them out of their comfort zone but they need to support the plan and keep their reservations to themselves or discuss them in private with you.

Finally, if they continue to be resistant, you may need to seriously consider if they should remain on your work team. If you've gone to all the effort outlined above and they are still unwilling to attempt to go along with the plan they could very well be poisoning the team in other areas. It may be time to part ways.

HABIT DEFINITION

The specific habit, including the cue and habit action, should be clearly defined and, if possible, illustrated for team members. If one member of the team is especially talented, he or she may be asked to design the official habit definition illustration. This may be provided on a sheet of paper to each team member and posted in a back room break room, office, or other common area where customers will not see it.

One approach is to have a team work session in which everyone on the team is given a sheet of paper and colored pencils and asked to illustrate the new habit.   These are then collected and posted in a rotating manner.

These illustrations should be creative.   The more creative they are the bigger the impression they will make.   They may be a single picture or comic strip style.

A single picture is easier to recall.   It may take some explanation so that people understand how it represents the habit and what they should recall about it each time they encounter the habit cue.   How might this look?   Thinking back to our original habit regarding turning on the "Available" light, there might be a picture of a check out station with a receipt printing on the left (the cue) and the team member flipping the switch on the Available light (the habit action).   As team members recall the picture, they associate the register printing the receipt with flipping the switch.   A colorful picture would be easy to recall.

Although the other part of the habit is not illustrated (turning off the light when the next customer approaches the register), there is likely enough here to serve as a good general reminder of the habit.   If the first part of the habit is adopted easily but cashiers are forgetting the other part of the habit (turning off the light) then another illustration could be designed showing this.   The two illustrations may be posted in different locations or rotated as needed.

The comic strip approach allows for an illustration of the entire habit in steps.   In this example, the first frame could be a close-up of the printer printing, the next of the cashier flipping the light switch on, the third frame the customer arriving at the register, and the fourth frame the cashier flipping the light switch off.   Add a comment or thought bubble above the customer's head thinking something like, *I'm going to come back here soon. They are very fast and efficient!*   This would nicely tie the habit to the reason it is being adopted and the broader objective.

While this is a thorough illustration, the team members would need to remember four images instead of just one.   The team preparing the reminders can decide what they feel would work bes— simpler and easy to remember (single image) or more detailed with a tie to the reason we are doing the habit (comic strip style).

Either way, habit descriptions work best when accompanied with illustrations instead of just words describing them. This is because illustrations are easier to remember and also are more quickly interpreted by your subconscious mind.

GOAL MEASUREMENT

Someone will likely need to work up tracking sheets or tick sheets. These may be easily done in Excel or Word using the table feature. Before beginning, it's a good idea to sketch out the design of the form and think through how much space each area may require.

At the top of the page the measure should be explained as well as a legend if there are various types of marks.   For example, here's how you might have designed a tracking sheet for the manager's check for cleanliness in our first scenario in the last chapter:

MANAGER CHECK SHEET FOR CLEANLINESS

Objective: Greatly improve the consistency and quality of cleaning surfaces in the restaurant so that you don't lose any points for this on the next inspection in three weeks.

Each hour, provide a grade for cleanliness of the counters and dining room based on the scale below. Any grade below "A" requires an explanation. The goal is all As.
- A: extremely clean with no sticky spots or crumbs anywhere
- B: very clean with only one or two missed spots
- C: clean but a few areas of sticky surfaces or crumbs
- D: several tables or large areas of the counter with sticky surfaces or crumbs
- F: it looks like there has been little to no effort to keep the counters and tables clean

Counters:

Time	Grade	Explanation
7am		
8am		
9am		
10am		
11am		
etc.		

Tables:

Time	Grade	Explanation
7am		
8am		
9am		
10am		
11am		
etc.		

Also keep in mind that most of the time these sheets will be posted for all team members to see. For this reason, they should be easy to understand and follow, even for people not recording measurements on them.

Individual tracking sheets, if part of the plan, may be designed in a similar manner. Be sure to include an explanation of how the sheet works and the goal they are working toward. When they compare the goal to their performance, they may quickly know how much more effort may be required.

Some of your measures may involve listing the top performers on the team. This serves as both recognition and to show other team members "the art of the possible". If Susan can perform the habit action consistently enough to be ranked in the first spot, it may inspire others to apply more effort and at least improve their current performance level. In addition, it is now a matter of pride for Susan to stay at the top of the list so she will continue working hard. Those further down the list will want to improve their rank by the next posting, so they will work hard as well.

You may show the "top 5", "top 10" or even list all the team members above average. Listing the performance level of all team members is another option, but, if you do, you may demoralize those ranked lower because the list is there for everyone to see. The result of this could be them giving up altogether or talking negatively about the habit improvement plan.   This list often works best when only the top performers or top half of performers are listed.

If the manager references the ranking when meeting with team members for coaching purposes, comparisons should be made to the team average or top quartile performance and not a comparison to specific individuals. Comparing one team member directly to a specific other team member may cause resentment between that team member and the team member with whom they are compared.

While some measures may be generated from a computer program, all will need to be noted somewhere.   Every measure should have some kind of tracking sheet.

Your tracking sheet may live in a computer program such as Excel, as long as it is printed or sent to team members from time to time so they may track habit consistency progress.

Your plan should include the name(s) of the team member or manager who writes on the tracking sheet, when and how often notes are made, and when and where it is posted. This tracking and feedback for team members is very important in the development of habits. Team members should look forward to seeing posted results and be able to expect that they will be posted on time.

SETTING UP THE REWARDS

Once the rewards are selected, they should be purchased or created.

The team leader who has access to funds should buy rewards that need to be purchased or authorize another team member to get them.

Some rewards may require a tracing sheet. For example, if an extra break is a reward, a sheet should be created to capture the date the reward is earned with another place to document when it is used.

Rewards may include recognition on a board or poster. Team members may create a special poster on which names and performance measures may be posted. Alternatively, a dry erase board with different color markers may be used if recognition is updated frequently.

If recognition is posted on an internet or intranet page, you will want to assign this to a team member who knows how to create the webpage or understands the procedure he needs to go through to get this created and updated.

If merchandise or a food item from the store or restaurant supply is earned by team members, it should also be tracked, just as you would track an extra break reward. The manager will likely have to account for these items in her inventory records.

Many times rewards may include a random draw. If this is the case, entries (whether they be tickets or just slips of paper) should be created and kept in a secure location. When team members get an entry, they may write their name on the slip of paper or ticket and put it into an entry box. This may be a simple shoe box with the top taped down and a slit in the top or it might be a glass jar or a more elaborate entry box. Whatever is used should be kept in a secure area. You don't want to have your habit development plan derailed because of doubts in regards to the validity of a draw.

Draws should be done in the presence of the team or at least several team members. Have fun with this. Do it in such a way as to build a couple of minutes of suspense. This is also a great opportunity to review the habit and emphasize why it is so important. Then have the name(s) drawn. Winners are then announced and names posted. Before the draw, a team member should design the winner sign or form that will be posted with a space to write in the winner's name. Post this immediately after the draw.

The Team Identity List should be created and posted in a special location. This is where habits, once engrained and executed consistently for a long period of time, are noted as part of what the team stands for and takes pride in. This is also the responsibility of the rewards team members to create and maintain.

All reward preparation should happen well before the first reward is earned. You can quickly lose momentum if a team member earns a reward but has to wait to receive it. You expect a lot of effort from team members in developing these habits. As a leader, you have to be very prompt in performing your responsibilities as outlined in the habit development plan. It's part of the example you are always setting for your team members, whether you realize it or not. If someone else on the team is assigned the task of rewarding team members but is not keeping up, you need to follow-up with them and make sure they provide the rewards promptly.

The posting of results and reward winners should also be done as soon as possible.   It is best to keep a running list. The more winners that are visible the more likely individual team members will feel they have a chance to win a reward. The other benefit is that team members naturally want to be like their peers. A long list of winners implies that almost everyone on the team is performing the habit action. The reluctant team member may then think, *If I want to feel like I'm part of this team, I need to start practicing the habit action too.*

HELPING TEAM MEMBERS WHO STRUGGLE WITH CONSISTENTLY COMPLETING THE HABIT ACTION

Helping adjust team member behavior will usually be the responsibility of the manager or team leader. However, team members may also be involved on occasion.

When a team member is failing to perform the habit action to the standards set by the team, the first thing the team leader should do is to meet with the team member in private, review her observations regarding the team member's lack of habit action follow through, and ask the team member what he thinks is preventing him from successfully completing the habit action consistently. In many cases, this one conversation may solve the problem by showing the team member the importance of following the habit development plan. Before the plan is implemented, the leader should think through how such a meeting would be handled.

The team leader should also think through possible challenges team members may encounter that may prevent them from consistently performing the habit action. For each challenge type, the team leader should figure out what approach she might take. These approaches will have to be customized based on the personalities involved, but the leader should have an idea of what her general approach might be. Here are some examples:

LACK OF SKILL IN A SPECIFIC AREA

If a team member is lacking specific skills, he may need to be trained, paired up with another team member for best practice training, or provided with an opportunity for practice until the skill may be fully developed.

Role playing might be a helpful way to practice the skill. Rehearse the habit with them (with the manager playing the part of the customer or another team member). Go through it a few times, even though the team member may feel that they understand after one time through it. A few times of going through it will reinforce the habit to the team member. Their heightened emotional state (which occurs naturally when role playing) will actually help the habit register even stronger.

LACK OF KNOWLEDGE IN A SPECIFIC AREA

The leader needs to determine what knowledge is required and figure out the best way to provide that knowledge to the team member. It is important that the leader makes the team member feel "safe" in admitting they lack knowledge and need some help. They may feel they are expected to have the relevant knowledge and fear frustrating the manager if they admit they don't have the knowledge. By making it safe for the team member to admit a need for knowledge, they will be more likely to bring it up and then the manager can provide what is needed to get the team member back on track.

THE TEAM MEMBER DOES NOT SEE VALUE IN THE HABIT

The leader needs to engage in the conversation with "on-the-fence" or "resistance" team members as previously covered. Without seeing value in the habit, the team member will likely consistently lag the rest of the team in performing the habit action.

THE CUE IS JUST NOT REGISTERING WITH THE TEAM MEMBER

The leader and team member may work together to think of an alternate cue that may remind the team member, or additional reminders may be created by that team member to remind himself. This is another situation in which it might make sense to pair this individual with a team member who has mastered habit development and may be able to provide best practice tips as to why she is able to consistently perform the habit action.

You may also coach the team member that when they see the cue they should also say to themselves the habit action. For example, they might say, "The receipt is printing, I need to turn on the light," and then they turn on the light. You are placing a thought between the action and the cue. This helps focus the team member's attention on the habit and increases the likelihood of their completing the habit action. Once it sufficiently becomes a habit, they no longer need to use the mental reminder.

THE TEAM MEMBER IS JUST NOT GIVING THE HABIT ENOUGH EFFORT

If the team member has the skills and knowledge to perform the habit, if they agree on the value of the habit and recognize the habit action cue whenever it occurs, yet they still don't follow through, the team leader may have to resort to disciplinary action. This may range from additional work assignments related to the habit or a documented discussion, to a verbal and even written reprimand. There may be a plan to make it a progressive disciplinary process if it does not have the desired impact. Disciplinary action of this type is usually done as a last resort and the need for it is often an indication that the team member has additional work related issues beyond not being able to follow the habit development plan.

CONTINGENCY PLANS

The team likely developed several contingency plans. Members of the team should take on the responsibility of making sure the team is ready to implement the contingency plans, if they become necessary.

This may include writing plans that may be followed if an anticipated challenge comes up. Many contingency plans require additional stocks of items in case there is an outage. These should be ordered and stored. Everyone on the team should know where these supplies reside.

Contingency plans may involve some research. You may need to identify another vendor, supplier, or repair service that may be quickly engaged. Remember to have a petty cash fund prepared and securely stored for a time when the business may need to make a quick purchase.

Finally, it is a good idea to have the contingency plans in a written form available to team members. In the initial habit training they don't necessarily need to be memorized by everyone, but it is good to review them so everyone on the team may have confidence that you have plans to overcome barriers.

REMINDERS

Members of the team should be assigned to create the habit action reminders. These reminders may be comprised of signs, table tops, stickers, or other printed material. They may also be programmed messages that appear on computer or Point of Sale screens. Team members working on the reminders need to know how to get these reminders programmed or at least know who to ask for assistance.

Other reminders are hand signals. If that is the case with this habit development plan, team members need to develop the hand signals and teach everyone on the team what they mean.

Reminders can be audio sounds, and the equipment needed for these needs to be purchased and set up. Other audio reminders may be in the form of spoken words. The reminder may need to be written as bullet points or a script that may be delivered by the team leader or team members.   Lists should be made that remind team leaders and team members at which team meetings the habit development plan should be promoted.

Team members who work on reminders should be encouraged to be creative. The more creative the reminder the more it will be noticed and recalled.   Use different fonts and different color ink. Make the signs in different colors and shapes. Make sure they are displayed in a very visible place for the team members for whom they are meant. Pictures are very memorable.   When possible, create pictures that communicate the habit reminder message.   Audio messages should also be memorable, creatively making use of various sounds, inflections, and storytelling.

Variety in your messaging will help keep it top of mind and not be taken for granted. When possible, change out signs on a regular basis to keep them fresh.   Develop different ways to word or picture the reminder message.   Make them humorous if possible.   The goal is to create reminders that are effective in reminding and motivating team members to perform the habit action when they experience the cue.

ACCOUNTABILITY PARTNERS

Think about how you want to assign accountability partners. The accountability partners are assigned for the entire time period of the habit development plan. Review schedules and see what makes sense.

If team members have overlapping schedules, they should be assigned to the same accountability team of two or three. This way they will be able to monitor and help each other follow through on habit actions. An explanation of how accountability teams work should be provided to the members of the accountability team. When roles are clearly defined up front, there is less chance that a team member will step out of bounds or another team member believe they have.

Here's an example of what such an explanation might look like for a server team focusing on providing consistent drink refills in a restaurant:

Refill Habit Development Plan: Accountability Partnerships

You and two other servers will help each other develop the habit of providing refills to guests before their glasses are empty.

Your role is to signal to your partner when you notice that a refill is needed. You may do this verbally ("refill on table 13") or cup your hand and then look at the table needing the refill, after you get your partner's attention.

We don't want our guests to have to wait so if your partner is not around and you have time, provide the refill yourself, but follow up with your partner. Remember, your partner cannot develop the habit if someone is constantly covering for them.

Do not get frustrated with your partner if they signal you when you have a table needing a refill. They are supposed to do that and are doing it to help you develop this habit. You should thank them for their help.

Finally, be sure to compliment your accountability partner at the end of the shift if they did not require any reminders.

ENVIRONMENTAL FACTORS

Team members should also review the list of environmental factors and determine what needs to be done before the team starts working on the habit development plan.   Having a conducive environment for habit development can mean the difference between success and failure, so the items on this list need to be implemented as planned. This will often mean having supplies related to the habit placed in very convenient locations for easy access.   It may mean that the team leaders need to reinforce job responsibilities such as the importance of keeping areas properly stocked.

Checklists are often used to make sure team members are following all steps of a process. These lists should be clear and easy to use with several copies available.   In addition, copies of the document should be saved on the computer so many team members know where they are and have quick access to them in case additional copies are used in the future.

Preparation for habit development should be done quickly by the team members.   Use deadlines to make sure this doesn't delay the launch of the new habit.

CHAPTER SUMMARY

Before you launch the new habit development plan, you will want the habit planning team to set the broader team up for success.

Now that your plan is created, you will need to assign plan tasks to team members. These include:
- Setting up the measurement system.
- Purchasing or creating rewards.
- Setting up for the contingency plans, in case any of them become necessary.
- Creating the reminders.
- Making the environmental adjustments.

Communicate the plan to the team and review the 13 elements of the habit development plan.

Team members typically fall into three categories:
1) Fully Supportive
2) On-The-Fence
3) Resistant

Convert the on-the-fence team members by asking questions about habit development, the team's habit building objective, and rewards.

Determine why the resistant team members are resistant.
- Understand why they don't support the habit development plan.
- Emphasize the need for the team to improve.
- If they continue to resist, you may need to seriously consider if they should remain on your work team.

Besides a simple definition, explain the habit in creative ways using illustrations.

Final important tasks include:
- Develop simple, clear, and easy to use tracking sheets.
- Prepare for rewards before they are needed and make sure they are provided promptly when earned.
- Help team members who struggle with adopting the habit.
- Set up contingency plans, reminders, and accountability partners.
- Adjust the environment to support habit development.

THE CRITICAL ROLE OF LEADERSHIP IN HABIT DEVELOPMENT ●┄┄

THERE ARE MANY FACTORS that will determine the success of your team habit development effort; none may be as important as leadership commitment.

A committed leader will figure out a way to make everything else happen. Without a committed leader, the team members who do care about the habit development plan will feel they are swimming upstream and will quickly become discouraged.

THE LEADER SETS THE TONE FOR THE TEAM

The work team culture is a reflection of the team leader's leadership style and personality. How the leader treats his or her team members is how they will treat their customers. If the leader is positive, respectful, and encouraging then most or all of the team members will treat their customers well.

There are many excellent books about the various aspects of leadership style so we won't delve too deeply into that here. However, for the purpose of habit development, it is useful to think about a very simple model of leadership that considers and contrasts two of the approaches to leadership:

- Command and Control Leaders give direction to their team and expect it to be followed. They rarely think through the impact of their actions on their teams. They make decisions without consulting with the team and often create "fire drills" and waste a lot of effort and time in the process. Team members are motivated by fear to do a good job. This leadership style can work and get things accomplished.
- Supportive Visionary Leaders provide vision to the team (the "what") and work with them to develop the process to achieve that vision (the "how"). These leaders consider how the team actions impact the team, their customers, and other teams with whom they work. They look for win/win scenarios. They define their job as "to provide the leadership and tools the team needs to take care of the customers." This leadership style is also effective in getting things accomplished.

As you've figured out by now, this book takes the approach of the Supportive Visionary Leader style.   When you are trying to shape people's subconscious habits through concentrated effort, you need a high level of genuine commitment. The Supportive Visionary Leadership style is most conducive to getting deeper commitment from team members and will lead to a lot more long-term success.

Let's cover some important behaviors of a Supportive Visionary Leader that relate to team habit development.

PROVIDE A VISION

Provide a clear vision to the team about what they will accomplish. The vision is a picture of where you see the team in the future. It does not have to be as precisely defined as a goal (following the SMART model), but it should be easy to understand and imagine.

The vision gives the team a destination. Having a team vision is important because it aligns the team to work together. Without it, team members will perform the basics. The team will just stagnate and not improve and grow. A vision challenges the team to move toward a specific point together. If you want to make improvements and for your team to create greater value, you must begin with a vision.

When you explain the vision you should include the "why" behind the vision and how it impacts customers, team members, suppliers, shareholders, and the community. What is in it for the team members? How does it impact your customers in such a way that they will do more business with you or become more loyal to you? What will this mean to the team? Why is it important? Is it something the team members will be really proud to help create? The vision should be exciting and motivational. It should be a stretch for the team to achieve, but should also be something that most members of the team believe is achievable. If not, you need to either change your vision or instill the confidence in your team that the vision is attainable. Without this belief by the majority of the team members, it will be a very slow and difficult journey.

Everyone on the team should be clear about the team vision. If you asked members of the team to describe their impression of the team vision, would all their answers be similar? If not, you have some additional communication and sharing to do. The vision should be revisited often. Team members should always be clear about the direction, and ultimate goal, they are working with others to achieve.

All initiatives and changes you make to your team processes should be tied to the vision. When team members propose ideas for the team, they should be judged based on how well they advance the team toward the vision.

Once everyone is clear on the vision, excited about it, and empowered to help advance the team toward it, you will be surprised at the progress that is possible.   If you don't make progress, you may need to revisit the vision to make sure it is well understood and that team members are excited about it.

Your team goal, which we've talked about previously, will flow from this vision.

Visions, while ideally the same for a long period of time, may need to be adjusted based on outside factors. A new competitor or competitive offering, a change in the customer base or customer preferences, a change in top company leadership, a change in technology, or new laws or regulations may cause you to rethink your vision.   It is fine to make a change, but be ready to explain the reasons for the change to the team.

Absent outside forces, your vision should remain constant for a long period of time.   If not, you'll be like the friends who rode in a car toward one destination then changed the destination to another place, and still another.   They didn't make any progress, they just rode around in circles and accomplished nothing.

INVOLVE THE TEAM IN DEVELOPING THE APPROACH

Although as a leader you likely have great ideas as to how you will achieve the vision, it is much better to provide the team members with the vision and get their thoughts on how to achieve it. They will likely come up with ideas you had not considered.   Some of them may not be as good as your approach, but others may be as good or better. Give each idea serious consideration and respect.   There are no bad ideas; however, some ideas are better than others.

After you provide the vision to the team, it may be a good idea to engage in a brainstorming session as we covered in a previous chapter. These sessions will generate great ideas that will help move the team toward the vision. Another big benefit is that it will get the team to really think through and focus on the vision. After conducting such a brainstorming session, it may be a good idea to mention the vision again and find out if any questions about the vision occurred to team members as they went through the brainstorming exercise. This may lead to additional, helpful dialogue about the vision.

When the team is discussing the best approach to achieving the vision, make sure the team focuses on ideas and not personalities. Some team members may see this as an opportunity to "score points" with the leadership team or make themselves look better than other team members. When you hear things like, "My idea is better than Bob's idea because..." then you need to be concerned that this is happening. Ideas under discussion should be named as an idea, not as someone's idea. For example, an idea should be called the "provide a money back guarantee to customers idea" rather than "Joe's idea."

If the team does talk too much about who came up with which idea then the wrong kind of emotions may seep into the discussion. Team members lose sight of judging the merits of an idea based on the idea itself, and instead judge it based on how much they like or don't like the person who proposed the idea. This may lead to discounting a great idea that was proposed by a less popular team member, or not fully vetting an idea suggested by a popular team member. The team suffers as a result, because they don't always select the best "how" to achieve the vision.

In the end, you must pick the best idea to achieve the vision, regardless of where it came from. Incorporating team member ideas into your plan to achieve the vision is very important because your team members will feel and be more committed. Why wouldn't they? We are using their ideas.

Take the time to convince the team. Of course, you are the leader and you have the final say as to how the team should proceed. You can do this by edict or explanation.   Edicts can lead to frustration and resistance, while explanation wins you respect.   Team members may not agree with you, but if your reasons are sound and they are rational, they will respect your different point of view and follow along more easily.

BE CREATIVE AND OPEN TO DIFFERENT APPROACHES

In the process of creating habit development plans, some team members will make some "out of the box" suggestions.   If you sense that it is an idea that other members of the team would support, do your best to figure out a way to incorporate it.   There will be some ideas that are simply not feasible because they may be contrary to long standing company policy that you know can't be changed or because they create undesirable side effects for your team, other teams, or the customers.

However, there will be ideas that you won't necessarily think would work.   Before you shut them down, you need to challenge your thinking.   Are you absolutely sure it would not work and be a mistake? Is there at least a possibility it might work?   If so, you need to approach the idea with a very open mind.   The teams that make the most and fastest progress are the ones that challenge conventional thinking.

Help mold the idea in such a way that it has the greatest chance of success.   At the end of the day, you are responsible for making sure the team makes the best choices.   If you truly have an open mind but strongly feel that a more conventional approach would be better, guide the team in that direction.

What if you reluctantly go along with an unconventional approach? How might you minimize risk and maximize learning from the experience?   The solution is to set it up as a pilot. Pilots are predefined as tests of an idea.   When you set up a pilot, you define what you wish to accomplish and you designate measures that you will use to evaluate the level of success.   Pilots may last any period of time and may be stopped early if they are not working. When you designate something as a pilot it often allows you to "bend the rules" since it is not a permanent change and you clearly state that you are not setting new precedence.   If the pilot works well, because you have evidence through your measures, you have a good chance of getting it approved permanently.

SEEK FIRST TO UNDERSTAND

As Stephen Covey said in his book, *The 7 Habits of Highly Effective People*, always seek first to understand.   If you are coaching a team member about a habit, first ask if there was a reason they did not perform the habit action.   Earlier we addressed the possibility of exceptions to the habit in cases when the habit might be detrimental to the customer experience.   First find out if there was a good reason that the team member did not do the habit.

Your team member may provide a reason. If they do, you'll need to determine whether the reason is good or not. If it is, compliment the team member for thinking through the situation and keeping her eyes focused on the ultimate goal, improving the customer experience.

If the reason is not valid, you'll want to explain to the team member why it was not a good reason to skip the habit action. You may have to ask him what he would do in a few other similar scenarios to make sure he is clear.   Make a mental or written note of the conversation so that, if the team member fails to perform the action in a similar situation in the future, you are able to address it appropriately.

REACT TO MISTAKES IN A CONSTRUCTIVE MANNER

When mistakes happen, the Supportive Visionary Leader does not focus on "punishment" but instead on understanding what happened, and how a similar mistake may be avoided in the future. That's not to say that there are not any consequences for mistakes, especially careless ones, but that should be of secondary importance.

This also applies to failure. If team members attempt to accomplish something and fail, even after giving it sufficient thought and effort, they should be praised for the attempt. A careful evaluation of what caused the failure should be conducted so the team can maximize the learning opportunity.   This also would involve a "knowing what we know now, how would we have approached that differently?" approach. When you learn valuable insights from a failure, it's not really a set-back but just part of the process of moving forward.

The more forgiving a leader is of first time mistakes the more he or she encourages risk taking among members of the team. Risk taking is an important quality for team members to have when they are working on creating more value.

In fact, if team members are performing flawlessly with no failure and no mistakes then there is a good chance they could advance toward the vision more quickly. We never seek mistakes or failure, but lack of them may be an indication of too much caution. This can slow progress.   If you think this is the case, first step back and assess yourself honestly in regards to how you deal with team failures and mistakes.   Do you react in such a way that may cause team members to be too cautious in the future?   If so, you might want to adjust your style.

If this isn't the case, consider having a conversation with team members about how the team might move more quickly toward the vision.   If they bring up fear of failure or mistakes if they move any faster, it would be a good opportunity to talk about your philosophy toward failure and "good failure" (failure as a result of a well thought out and high effort attempt).   Point out that if the team experienced a little more "good failure" they could very well move more quickly toward the vision.

This applies to habit development as well.   If everyone on the team easily reaches the milestones and if, in fact, the team achieves the goal weeks ahead of schedule, it would be a good idea to challenge the team more by selecting another habit to develop. However, if you do this too soon, the current habit may not be fully set in the culture and then you've created a problem. It's important to balance the challenge to the team.

PROVIDE RECOGNITION AND APPRECIATION

Provide recognition and appreciation for doing a great job in public, while providing discipline in private. The only exception to this is for the shy team member who does not like to be recognized in front of the team and a good leader will respect this.

Disciplinary actions such as performance discussions and reprimands should happen in private and should not be shared with other members of the team. This does not apply to minor "reminders" about following the new habit. In many cases, this will happen in front of other team members, but it should be a quick reminder (e.g. "Please remember to…") and not a disciplinary discussion (e.g. "That's the fourth time today you've forgotten to… You forget again and I'm writing you up!").

Look for opportunities to provide genuine recognition to your team members. Recognition, even in the form of a kind word, can have a profound impact on team members. It provides an emotional lift and encourages even more great performance.

Recognition may also come in the form of sharing positive comments about the team or team member from other people. If your team receives praise from senior leadership, be sure to share it with them. If you receive customer feedback in the form of conversations with customers, survey results, submitted comments or observations from other members of the staff, be sure to share the feedback with the relevant team members. This feedback is very meaningful. One positive customer comment can make a team member's day. Beyond the good feeling it brings, the feedback helps others see what actions and effort lead to positive customer experiences and encourages them to model the behavior.

The habit development plan will often include rewards and recognition that will be provided by the team leader. Be prompt and genuine when you deliver the rewards and recognition.

STAY POSITIVE AND ENTHUSIASTIC

When possible, the team leaders should communicate and interact in a positive tone. Look first for the good before pointing out opportunities. When problems arise, put them into proper perspective and look at the potential benefits to the team of overcoming them or acknowledge that things could have been even more challenging.

At the same time, the leader should not sugar-coat serious issues. A good leader is both positive and pragmatic. If there are obvious challenges the team is facing that the leader does not acknowledge, the team may lose faith in the leader's ability to lead the team through the challenges. Great Supportive Visionary Leaders present challenges in a positive, motivating way. Here are some examples:
- Too Positive/Not Pragmatic: "This issue is no big deal. We should just ignore it."
- Too Negative: "This issue is very concerning. It may very well be impossible to overcome. I am not sure how we'll do it."
- Supportive Visionary Leader: "Yes, this is a serious challenge but I know our team is up to it and am very confident we will find a solution to overcome this. Let's start brainstorming some creative options."

As well as being positive, a leader should be enthusiastic about the team vision, the team accomplishments, and the team progress. This enthusiasm reveals the level of care that the leader has for the team and the vision.

It's been said that "enthusiasm is contagious" and it often seems that way. Be that high energy leader who inspires the team; even if it means you have to step out of your comfort zone a bit. Practice ahead of time what you plan to say to your team in meetings. The time you have in front of your team is a precious opportunity to influence and inspire.   Make sure you are fully prepared and enthusiastic before every session. Let your passion for the team vision show.

If, as a leader, you don't feel enthusiastic about the vision you have for your team, you may need to spend more time understanding the value and importance of the vision.   Either that, or cultivate a vision you can be genuinely enthusiastic about.

For a habit development plan to be successful, it must have the full support of the leadership team.   All leaders should talk about it often in a very positive, encouraging, and enthusiastic tone.   Back up your talk with action. Demonstrate, through words and deeds, how much you value the habit development plan and your team's efforts to follow through with it.

BUILD TRUST AND BE TRANSPARENT WITH YOUR TEAM

Trust between team members and the team leader and trust between the team members is a requirement if you want your team to reach its full potential. The team leader sets the example.

Supportive Visionary Leaders shoot straight with the team.   If there are risks, the leader is clear with the team and communicates the risks to them with a balanced, realistic perspective.   He or she acknowledges great team performance, but also points out any areas in which the team is underperforming.

When working with new team members, the leader's best approach is to assume she can trust them and that they have good will intended. Until and unless there is ample evidence to the contrary, the leader should assume team members are doing their best and are motivated to do what is best for the team, the customers, and other stakeholders.   Treating someone in this manner from the start will encourage them to live up to the trust and the respect you have toward them.

When their behavior deviates from the trust you've placed in them it should not be ignored. Catch it early and address it right away. Give them the benefit of the doubt and assume good intentions but really "seek to understand" (as Stephen Covey would put it). If they cannot provide a good explanation for behaving contrary to the team vision, you need to find out what you can do to help them get back on track. Is additional training required? Are they not tapped into regular information they need to be able to do their job well? Whatever the case, do what you can to help. However, if they continue to be uncooperative, it may be time to have a conversation about how some roles are better than others based on the person's skills, knowledge, and work preferences, and that maybe this isn't the right role for them.

You should focus your comments and coaching on behavior—not the attitude that you perceive they have. There are two reasons—first, behavior is what you are paying them for. Behavior does include an important element of quality. Chances are, if they don't have the right attitude, it will become evident in the lack of quality of their behavior. Talk in terms of that when you are coaching them. Addressing your perceptions about their attitude is a losing move on your part. They will insist their attitude is fine. Since attitude itself is not visible, you can't argue that point. All you can do is point to behavior and insist they meet or exceed the team standards.

Remember that every team member is an individual and they process feedback much differently. Some team members need to be handled delicately because they may be very sensitive. A coaching discussion with them may be framed up as extremely positive about the job they are doing except for this one little area where they need to focus. These team members get the message quickly and completely and nothing more needs to be said. Other team members need a much more serious coaching session, barely mentioning the positive and focusing heavily on the negative to even begin to motivate them to make a change. Most team members are somewhere in between these two extremes. If you wish to effectively motivate everyone on your team, you'll need to understand the best approach for each team member.

It is important to apply these principles when you are coaching team members about the habit development plan. Trust the team members' commitment to the plan. Expect that they intend to follow through consistently with the habit action. If they fail, chalk it up to "human failings" and help them get back on track. Be transparent with the team about the progress they are making on the habit development plan. Praise them when they are following the plan well. Express your disappointment and assist them if they are struggling due to lack of effort and focus.

It is a good idea to document your coaching sessions with your team members. Write a short list of bullet points—what you talked to them about, what was discussed, and the outcome. This way, if future coaching is required, you can reference the earlier meeting (e.g., "Sam, we met two weeks ago and discussed the habit development plan. You committed to follow it, yet we both agree you haven't. What can we do differently so you will follow it in the future?"). Just knowing you are tracking what was discussed can be motivating to team members. If the team members have a company email, it is a good practice to send a copy of your bullet points to your team member to reinforce your discussion and to reinforce commitments made by the team member. If they have no company email it might make sense to provide a printed copy. At the end of your bullet points you can ask him to meet with you if he has any additional questions or needs additional training.

BE EMOTIONALLY SELF-AWARE

Understand the importance of being aware of your own emotions. Good Supportive Visionary Leaders have a good sense of how they feel and are able to keep their emotions under control. They know they are best at coaching team members when they are not feeling emotionally charged. They understand the importance of timing, and do not engage in a performance conversation with a team member until they are certain that they are prepared to make it productive.

Notice your emotional state during the course of the day. If you pay close attention, you should be able to notice patterns. What times of the day do you tend to be in a good mood and in full control of your emotions? What times of the day do you feel down, annoyed or irritated? When working closely with team members it is best to plan ahead to leverage the times of the day you are at your emotional best.

Be aware of how you come across to others. If you are fortunate, someone may provide insightful feedback to you about how your approach impacts them and the team. However, even when feedback is requested, few team members will speak up to offer their leader constructive feedback on improvement opportunities. Since this is the case, if you wish to support your team better, you need to carefully observe how they react to your approach to various situations. If you consciously observe their body language and facial expressions, you can often figure out what works well and what doesn't. When doing this, you must keep in mind that everyone is different and that some people will react positively and others negatively based on the same behavior you may display with them.

Habit development can test your patience, especially if the habit seems very easy to you yet a few team members are not following it. Make sure your coaching of these team members is productive. Remember that your objective is not to "punish them" but to get them to follow the habit development plan. It is much easier to do this if you coach them when the timing is right and you are in the right emotional state of mind.

THE TEAM HABIT DEVELOPMENT PLAN REQUIRES YOU TO BE VIGILANT

Many fully committed team leaders will have to step out of their comfort zone and be very strict about following the new habit themselves and holding team members accountable for following it.

There will be high pressure situations in which they need to stay focused on making sure the habit development plan is being executed.

There will come many occasions when you are in a hurry and pass by a team member not consistently practicing the habit.   These are moments of truth in which the team leader must stop and coach the team member to follow the habit.   If the team leader walks by without addressing it, it is as if they are saying, "You know this habit development plan we've been discussing and all the reasons it is important?   Between you and me, I'm just not that committed to it and if, as a team member, you want to pass on doing it sometimes, it is okay with me!"   As you can imagine, when this happens, the habit development plan is put in jeopardy.   If this continues day after day, the plan will die.

How frustrating would this be for the team members who were committed to the new habit and put a lot of effort into the development of it?   To see it fail because their leader did not put forth enough effort would be very disappointing and have a very negative impact on their morale.   These are your really good, committed team members. Don't let them down.

SHARE THE SPOTLIGHT

Even though, as the leader, you are the most important single individual responsible for the success of the habit development plan, you must generously credit the team when the plan is a success. Make them the "stars" of the success and lavish as much sincere, public praise as possible. Besides being the right thing to do, this will make the next habit development plan easier to develop and execute. It takes belief in the habit development process for it to become part of a team's culture.   Nothing helps instill this belief more than experienced success.

Let others in the company know of the team's success.   Share the key measures as proof. Even though you are giving the team full credit, others will know that it was your great supportive visionary leadership that led to success.

SELF-EVALUATION

As the leader, you have to demonstrate more discipline than anyone on the team in performing your role in the habit development plan. You may consider setting up your responsibilities in the team habit development plan as personal habits you develop.

If you do, you will set up goals for yourself and your fellow leaders with tracking and rewards. Here are a few example goals:
- Fill out team habit development tracking sheet each day (or each hour if that is what is required).
- Verbally provide feedback to at least five team members per day (either compliments for following the team habit development plan or coaching on how to do better).
- Emphasize the importance of the team habit development plan at every team meeting.
- Provide the individual team member rewards the same day they earn the reward.
- Document all habit development coaching sessions with team members.

If you feel you don't formally need to establish a set of habits for yourself, you could instead do a daily evaluation. Simply make a list of all your responsibilities related to the team habit development plan. This includes what you are supposed to do and when you should complete it. Make a tracking list of these responsibilities.

At the end of every workday, pull out the list. For each item, ask yourself:
- Did I perform this task? If yes, make a mark on your tracking sheet for this day.
- What about my performance was really good? Did I have a very successful coaching session? Did I make sure the team

consistently practiced the habit, even through a very
challenging work day?
- What about my performance was lacking? Did I look the other
way when team members missed doing the habit action?   Did I
fail to prepare for a coaching session and as a result it did not
go very well?
- What can I do better tomorrow?   What do I want to commit to
so I'll be a better leader tomorrow?   What specific plans might I
make for the next day?   Should I put a coaching session or two
on my calendar for team members who are not following
through on the habit development plan?

CHAPTER SUMMARY

Leadership commitment is the most important factor in implementing
a successful habit development plan.
- The leader sets the tone for the team.

Types of leaders:
1) Command and Control Leaders give directions and expect them
   to be followed.
2) Supportive Visionary Leaders provide vision to the team and
   work with the team to develop the process to achieve the
   vision.

A vision is where you see the team in the future.
- It aligns the team to work together.
- Team members need to clearly understand the "why" behind
  the vision.
- Team goals flow from the vision.

Involve the team in planning how to achieve the vision.
- Be creative and open to different approaches.
- If you disagree, challenge your thinking.
- In the end, guide the team to the idea that has the greatest
  chance of success.

React to mistakes in a constructive manner.
- Instead of focusing on "punishment", focus on avoiding the mistake in the future.

Provide recognition and appreciation.
- Praise in public and discipline in private.
- Look for opportunities to provide encouraging recognition to your team members.

Stay positive and enthusiastic.
- Openly discuss challenges, but portray optimism that "with hard work from the team, we can overcome them."
- Be that high energy leader who inspires the team, even if it means you have to step out of your comfort zone a bit.

Build trust and be transparent with your team.
- Communicate risks with a balanced, realistic perspective.
- Assume good intentions by team members.
- Focus your comments and coaching on behavior—not the attitude that you perceive they have.

Be emotionally self-aware.
- Notice the impact your approach has on members of the team.

Vigilantly follow the habit development plan.
- Be very consistent in coaching team members to stick to the plan—every time.

Share the spotlight with the team.
- When your team enjoys success, lavish as much sincere, public praise as possible.

Evaluate yourself daily on how well you are performing your role in the habit development plan and supporting your team.

LAUNCH THE HABIT AND MAKE IT A WAY OF LIFE •⋯

HABIT LAUNCH

THE TEAM HAS ACCOMPLISHED a lot.   The habit development plan has been written with a clear definition of the habit, the team has been trained, performance tracking is in place, and the team is clear on the goal, milestones and rewards.   Plans and resources are in place to handle contingencies, provide reminders, and create an environment that will help make habit development successful. Accountability partners have been assigned and the roles are clear. The management team is clear about their very important role in the habit development plan.

With everything now in place, it is time to launch the habit.   This happens on the pre-defined launch date.   On that day, when team members arrive at work, they should be reminded that today is the beginning of the habit development launch and the team leadership should very actively monitor the habit during the day.

The first few days of habit development are critical. There are two types of forces at play:

1) Empowering Forces: Because team members see the value in the new habit and ideally have a positive attitude toward it, there is energy and a certain level of enthusiasm directed toward it. This is very helpful. If leveraged properly it will lead to momentum in the development of the habit.

2) Challenging Forces: However, implementing a new habit is hardest at the beginning because it must be done fully with the conscious mind. The team is forging a new path. It's like going into a forest without a path. On the first day, they are cutting that path. If the path is cleared well and straight, the next day it will be a little easier to follow. Day after day of following the new habit will help the subconscious takeover from the conscious mind in performing the habit action when it is triggered by the cue. Even after several days of practicing a new habit there continues to be a built in resistance to the new habit that must be overcome.

The trick is to make sure the empowering forces are stronger than the challenging forces.   Both types of forces are strongest on the first day. If the empowering forces stay relatively stronger than the challenging forces, the habit will be a success.

Without proper attention and effort, however, the empowering forces lose their power quicker than the challenging forces and the habit never fully develops to the level of consistency the team originally intended.

Imagine what it would be like to go through all the effort of training the team about habits, developing a habit action plan, and creating all the important elements, only to have it fade away.

It is this reason that the team and team leadership must be fully committed to making the habit work. They must take a "no excuses" attitude.   Although there will be unanticipated challenges, they must be confident in their ability to overcome any barrier and remain fully committed to successfully implement the habit and make it a permanent part of the team's identity.

The first few days set the tone.   These are the moments when choices will be made by leaders and team members alike that will ultimately determine the fate of the habit development plan.

If team members are fully committed and consciously focus on practicing the habit they will contribute to a positive habit development environment. They cannot compromise or take shortcuts.   When faced with the option to "skip the habit just this once," they need to remain committed and choose to perform the habit.   Over several days or a few weeks they will begin setting the habit up to be taken in by the subconscious mind and it will become easier and easier.

As members of two to three person accountability partner teams, accountability partners need to take their roles seriously and help each other be successful. Whether it is helping remind team members when they forget to practice the habit action, or just a debrief from time to time regarding what is and is not working, they must live up to their expected role early on.

Team leaders, especially at the very beginning of the habit development plan, will drive the level of success based on their commitment and follow through.   They must constantly communicate the importance of the habit development plan—verbally in every meeting and in non-verbal ways such as obviously and constantly monitoring the team to make sure they are following the habit development plan.

Launching a habit is not unlike the launch of a rocket.   There are many systems that must be prepared and working properly.   These are your plans, goals, milestones, tracking, rewards, and reminders, how you will handle team members who are not adopting to the new habit, your contingency plans, accountability teams, and the environmental factors you have adjusted to enhance habit development.   If any of these systems are faulty, your habit development plan is at risk.   That's why we've spent so much time in the past two chapters discussing preparation for habit launch.

Also similar to launching a rocket, launching a habit requires a lot of energy and work in the beginning. These are the more critical moments in which enough momentum must be built to escape the "gradational pull" of the team's collective subconscious resistance to change.   Only constant, conscious effort will overcome that.

But in time, like a rocket, momentum will build. The habit will become more and more consistent. As it does, it will become much easier to practice.

HABIT DEVELOPMENT TEAM CHECK-IN

The habit development team should meet after the first week to review results and determine how well the plan is working. Ahead of the meeting, the team should reach out to the broader team and gather feedback on what is working well or not well with the habit development plan.   You might even ask members of the broader team to share their thoughts with planning team members to make sure everyone on the broader team is represented.

In addition, if the team has a suggestion box or some other way for team members to provide feedback, that should be utilized as well.   If accountability partners are meeting, they should discuss and write down thoughts as to what is working well and what might need to be adjusted. Finally, the manager should seek feedback and carefully observe how well the plan is working.

If the habit development deployment gets off to a bad start, the team that designed the plan needs to determine the root cause for the poor start.

Begin with measurement results. Look for patterns. Are there days of the week, specific shifts, or common circumstances that occur just before habits are missed? If you charted results, would you find that the team got off to a great start only to fade?   This is very common when people are developing new habits.   This points to the need for more consistent monitoring, reminders, and communication about the importance of the habit.   Managers need to be more active in coaching team members to perform the habit.

If there are common circumstances that seem to lead to habit action failure, determine contingency plans for these in the future. Then take the time to teach the team about the best way to handle them. Follow-up with close monitoring and you'll very likely see improvement.

If the pattern reveals specific shifts, the manager in charge of that shift likely needs to step up.   First make sure he understands the importance of the habit. Then determine if he is comfortable coaching team members and calling them out when they miss performing the habit.   Make sure he sets a good example by following through on the habit action every time he is in a position to do it, and never ignores the failure of a team member to perform the habit.   These things must be consistently addressed for the habit to be consistently practiced.

In addition, you should gather feedback from team members. Here are some possible obstacles and some ways to overcome them:

IF TEAM MEMBERS ARE UNCLEAR ABOUT THE HABIT OBJECTIVE

First determine what the habit planning team members think the objective is and how important they think it is.   Do this by just asking them to explain it as if you were a brand new team member.   If it is very different than the intended objective, try to figure out how team members got the wrong impression. Determine a different approach to explain the objective.   Then meet with the broad team (or talk to them individually) and review the objective in a different way. Make sure they are clear by having some team members repeat back what they believe the objective to be.

IF TEAM MEMBERS ARE UNCLEAR ABOUT THE HABIT DEFINITION

You will handle this similarly to how you would handle a misunderstanding about the objective. Begin by asking members of the team to tell you how the habit works. Make sure they talk about the cue, the habit action, the tracking, and the rewards. If their answer is lacking, redefine the habit for them, emphasizing the part they were missing.

IF THE TEAM IS NOT CONSISTENTLY TRACKING PERFORMANCE

Find out from the habit planning team why they think the team is not using the measurement tracking sheets to track progress. Are the tracking sheets getting lost? Is the system set up in such a way that they are expected to fill out a tracking sheet at the same time as they are undertaking another critical task? Is there a better place to keep them or post them? Are self-tracking team members forgetting to fill out the sheet? What can management do differently to remind them of the importance of tracking at the beginning of their shift, and make sure they filled out their tracking sheet by the end of their shift?

Is management failing to keep track of performance? If so, consider an "incentive" to help them remember. This could be reminders from the team or even requiring the forgetful manager to bring in a box of doughnuts for the team the next time she works.

IF THE TEAM IS UNCLEAR ABOUT THE GOAL OR GOAL MILESTONES

Individually ask team members to identify the goal and goal milestones.   If they are unsure or incorrect, remind them of the goal and milestones.   Follow-up with these team members the next day to make sure they have remembered.   If they understand the measurements, they should be able to easily recall the goal.

IF THE TEAM OR INDIVIDUAL REWARDS ARE NOT BEING AWARDED

First make sure the rewards are readily available.   Then think through the distribution of rewards and adjust the system so the managers or team members awarding the rewards may do so consistently.

IF THE TEAM OR INDIVIDUAL REWARDS ARE NOT MOTIVATING

If the habit planning team feels that the habits are not motivating based on what they've heard from other team members, revisit the rewards.   Although the objective and reason behind the objective should be the primary motivation to adopting the habit, the rewards should be helpful in motivating the team members.

Rewards are part of the habit development model and have their place, especially in the beginning.   If they seem to be ineffective, the habit planning team may need to develop alternate rewards to try.

IF THE TEAM'S BAD HABITS ARE SO STRONG THEY ARE OVERRIDING THE NEW, GOOD HABIT

Make sure both the old bad and new good habit are triggered from the same cue.   If not, you may need to redesign the cue part of the habit definition.   If the bad habit does launch from the same cue, you need to get your team members to be more aware and pay closer attention when the cue triggers a response. Are the reasons for changing to the new habit strong enough?   If not, make them stronger and talk about them more often.

If the reasons for change are due to lack of concentration, the habit planning team needs to figure out what might be done to draw more attention to the cue. You may institute a "pre-habit" thought that is triggered by the cue.   The thought is simply acknowledging the cue and what the team member should be doing. Since having a thought is easier than performing a habit action, this may help the team member focus on the cue and their expected habit action.

IF THE TEAM MEMBERS ARE MISSING THE CUES ALTOGETHER

Habit planning team members should meet and discuss the possible reasons that the reminders are being missed. Then they may make adjustments to the reminder locations or to the reminders themselves.

The team may also work to focus more on linking the cue to the habit action. Are they being reminded at the beginning of every shift?   Is management keeping an eye on the operation and alerting team members when a cue fails to trigger the habit action?   What is distracting the team members from noticing the cue and linking it to the habit behavior? Answers to these questions will lead to a solution.

IF THE ACCOUNTABILITY PARTNERS ARE NOT HELPING EACH OTHER BE SUCCESSFUL

Did you clearly review the roles so each partner knows what's expected of them, including providing feedback and assistance and accepting feedback from the other partner as helpful and coming from a place of good intentions?   Should these roles be reviewed in the larger team meeting as a reminder from time to time?   Do you allow a few minutes for the accountability partners to meet and exchange habit-building best practice techniques?   Is there a personality conflict that needs to be addressed? Are there partners that are not approaching it from a place of good intentions?   How can you help them adjust their approach so they are trying to be helpful to their accountability partner and not using the opportunity to put them down?

IF THE ENVIRONMENTAL FACTORS ARE TOO DISTRACTING OR SERVE AS BARRIERS

What are the reasons that team members give for not following through on the habit action? Are there barriers to the habit action plan that the planning team failed to identify? Do they need to create plans to address these barriers?   As you begin to implement the action development plan, are there other ideas about adjustments that may be made to the environment that may assist with habit development that you had not previously considered?

MAKING ADJUSTMENTS

It is likely that, after evaluating performance at the end of the first week, the team will make some adjustments to the plan. This is to be expected.   The team should think through these changes carefully to make sure they minimize the need for additional adjustments in the near term.

The team needs to develop a solid communications plan to share these adjustments with the broader team so they do not create confusion.

SECOND WEEK'S REVIEW MEETING

After the second week of habit development the habit development planning team should meet and review progress.   Additional adjustments may be considered.   Then the team needs to weigh the benefit of these adjustments against the confusion that additional adjustments may cause.

If the team habit development is running according to plan and milestones are being successfully met, the planning team may provide communication to the broader team that encourages them to keep up the good work. The planning team may choose to skip a week before meeting again.

CONSISTENCY IS THE FOCUS

As the team applies the habit development plan, the focus should be on consistent habit action execution. The more consistent the team is in performing the habit action, the quicker it will become an engrained habit and the easier it will be to perform the habit action with each successive cue.

Consistency is most effectively built when no exceptions are allowed. Some team members will feel this is very picky and want to provide reasons for special exceptions from time to time. Each exception, however, sets habit development back because it causes the subconscious mind to change direction and lose momentum. It's as if every successful execution of the habit is one step forward and each exception is three steps back. The fastest way to proceed forward is to avoid exceptions.

HANDLING DISRUPTIONS

There will be disruptions from time to time. These are not the daily resistance some team members may have in practicing the habit action. Disruptions are major interruptions to the normal course of the work procedures that the team follows. They may be an emergency, a sudden adjustment needed to accommodate a customer's needs, or in an extreme case of being understaffed.

All of these scenarios are likely accounted for in your contingency plan so you'll know how to handle them in the moment, if they should arise.

After the "crisis" passes, however, the team is very vulnerable to losing momentum. It is at this point that the leaders and team should look back at the first few days of the habit development plan in which extra focus was placed on the plan's execution. Returning to this level of focus will help the team transition back into practicing the habit action with very little loss of momentum.

REACHING THE GOAL

If the team habit development plan is sound, when the team reaches the goal, the habit will be automatic to most members of the team. Their subconscious minds will take over whenever they encounter the cue and the habit action will flow naturally and easily.

The broad team and habit development planning team can be proud that they have successfully improved the customer experience. Besides the rewards that the team may have designated for this point in time, the leadership should meet with the team members and acknowledge the success. They should once again tie the habit to the positive impact on the customers, team members, and the operation.

TEAM IDENTITY

Becoming consistent with the habit is very important. Equally important to long-term practice of the habit is changing how the team and individual members of the team think about themselves. They need to see themselves as professionals who always practice the habit. They need to believe they have a reputation for it and that when people talk about the team, it is one of the ways people describe it.

An example is Walt Disney World cast members. They have an identity, built over the years, of being friendly to guests. On everyone's first day of work, they attend a class called Traditions. One of the things these new team members take away from the class is that being friendly and helpful to guests is a company identity. It is expected of everyone on the team.   Since these new cast members are now part of the company, most of them start embracing this identity themselves.   This is a great example of how much a company can accomplish when good habits are purposefully established, practiced, and expected.

At this point the habit that the team just successfully adopted should be added to the official team identity. This is a list of what the team stands for and does.   Items on the list must be proven so the entire list is respected and believed. This list becomes an important piece of the training of new team members and should be reviewed with current team members on a regular basis.

It's a good idea to have the list posted in a prominent location and used whenever coaching takes place related to one of the items on the list.

NEW TEAM MEMBER TRAINING

Over time your business will hire new team members.   Any habits the team has developed should be covered explicitly in training.   Trainers should share the stories behind the habit development. This accomplishes two things. New team members will appreciate the importance of the habit when they hear how much effort was invested in establishing the habit.   They will also begin to understand the habit development planning process. This is important because they will participate in the next habit development plan the team chooses.

Part of the new team member check out evaluation should include any new habits the team has developed.   If this isn't done, new team members won't follow the habit, the veteran team members will see this and assume the habit is not as important and, in time, the habit will become inconsistently practiced.   All that work in developing the habit will be wasted.

When interviewing prospective new team members, it would be prudent to share a little about the habit development process with them and talk about how the team is always working hard to continuously improve the customer experience. The reaction from the job candidate may help the hiring manager in making the hiring decision. New team members who are not interested in continuous improvement would only put a drag on successful teams that are regularly adding new habits to improve the customer experience.

When selecting your training staff, make sure you pick team members who are 100% committed to the habit development plans that the team has implemented. These team members should be extremely consistent with the habits you've established. Too many trainers, especially in service businesses, train new team members in two parts. First they review how the team member should do the work based on the company standard operating procedures. Then they show the new team members other ways of doing things and the habits everyone seems to practice.

If they are more efficient, alternative ways of doing things are great. But if they make sense, they should be part of the standard training. Usually, there are reasons the company does not want team members doing things these other ways.

Monitor your trainers carefully. Make sure they are teaching the important habits the way they are intended and that they are monitoring new team member performance to make sure they are following them. If not, you should address this with your trainers. If they still are not teaching the habits properly, you may need to consider getting new trainers. It's that important.

New team members should be trained on the habit in much the same manner as the habit development plan. Take them through the habit development training (chapter 3). Talk about objectives; why the habits are important, and habit cues. Establish habit tracking metrics, and keep doing them for at least a couple of weeks after the habit seems well adopted by the new team member. Consider setting up a temporary habit reward plan for these new team members, even if you've moved past the need for rewards for the rest of the team. Review contingency plans and set up reminders for these team members. Establish accountability partners who will help them stay on track when the trainer and manager are not around. Point out the environmental factors that were designed to support habit development.

This will all be relatively easy if it is a habit the team has developed. Your trainer can just use the original habit development plan, adjusting it as necessary.

There is a side benefit any time you train new team members. Existing team members will see them training on the habits, and may even be involved as accountability partners. This will help reinforce the habit to everyone on the team.

IF YOU ARE STARTING A NEW BUSINESS

If you happen to be starting a new business from scratch, you will find you have an advantage over existing businesses in establishing good habits. Existing businesses have to overcome bad habits and the status quo.   If you think of establishing a new habit as setting a new path, existing businesses have to pull people from the established paths. New businesses set the path from the start.

Although new businesses will be hiring team members who may have picked up bad habits from other locations, the new environment of your business will make that habit less relevant. The cues will be somewhat different in your business. These team members who previously did not have good habits may initially struggle more than your new team members who never worked in this type of business before. However, with effort and attention, all team members can quickly adopt to the habits you work to establish.

For these reasons, starting a new business, or opening a new location of an existing business is a great opportunity. However, there is one additional challenge. As the manager of a new business, you'll need to think through all habits you want the team to practice up front and make them a part of the training. Any areas you don't think of will naturally and almost randomly evolve into habits. Usually, naturally evolving habits are not nearly as good as planned habits, and are not nearly as consistent. Taking time to carefully process map and think through every step your team members will go through to deliver great experiences for your customers will be time well invested.

ONGOING

Any good habit should be monitored to ensure it is well maintained. From time to time, related measures should be reviewed. Pull that habit's development plan and compare current performance to that habit's goal. You should be consistently achieving it. If it appears that habit consistency is waning, it may be time to revisit the habit.

If caught early enough, you won't have to start from scratch. Immediate focus on the habit may get the team back on track quickly. This is kind of a "back to the basics" approach. If the habit is not picked back up quickly, you may need to reinstate a habit development plan.

The first habit will take the most effort because the team has never been through the process before. Each successive habit development process will become easier. At this point, the team must guard against complacency and taking shortcuts. If they leave some of the elements of the process out, they risk being less successful in their habit development effort. Use the steps outlined in this book.

If the team stays consistent in the way they approach habit development, the team will become proficient at making positive, lasting change. This is the ultimate skill for the team to develop.

Over time, your team may add several habits to your team identity list. Each time this is done, you are improving the customer experience in some way. This will give you and your team a competitive advantage and most likely lead to business growth.

DON'T STOP AFTER YOUR FIRST SUCCESS

After your first habit development success you may be tempted to celebrate success and take a break before beginning work on your next habit. If you do, you'll lose some of the momentum you've begun to build.

The best time to launch a new habit is when you celebrate the success of the one you just finished. The team members are likely happy and proud of themselves. Leverage this energy in building excitement for the next new habit. Announce the habit objective and when the habit development team will meet to begin work on it. This is a good time to remind the team that it is important they don't lose sight of the habit they just successfully established. They will need to maintain that while adding the new habit.   They've learned how to successfully juggle one ball, now it is time to move on to two.

Follow the process outlined in this book again. Don't shortcut it. It will be easier because your team members will now be familiar with the habit development process. Go back to your research. If nothing significant has changed in the market since you researched and process mapped your business from the customer and team member perspectives, you can just review it and select an objective for the team to work on.

Give this objective to the habit development team and let them go to work defining it, setting goals and goal milestones, developing tracking systems and rewards, describing action to be taken based on substandard performance, identifying bad habits this may be replacing, developing the action contingency plans and a system of reminders, establishing the roles of accountability partners, and developing ideas to create a supportive environment for the development of the new habit. If you want to continue being successful, you cannot skip steps in this process.   It is the quickest, most efficient and effective way to establish consistent long-term habits in your team.

When this second new habit is celebrated, kick off the next one, or even try two new habits at once. They may be separate or tied together with the first one serving as a cue for the second one.   For example, a pool cleaner may have an initial cue of finishing cleaning the pool. This cues him or her to leave a note for the owners, letting them know when it will be safe to swim again. Finishing this note cues a second new habit of sweeping off the pool deck if he or she tracked any dirt or mud on it.

THE ULTIMATE GOAL: A TEAM THAT SUCCESSFULLY PRACTICES CONTINUOUS IMPROVEMENT

Each time your team successfully completes a habit development plan, they will become more and more proficient with continuous improvement. Visualize this state for your team and you will agree that this would create a very important competitive advantage for your business.   This is in addition to the competitive advantage you've established along the way with the addition of each new habit that contributes to a better customer experience.

Now, go develop great habits!

CHAPTER SUMMARY

The first few days of habit development are critical. Two forces are at play:
- Empowering forces that contribute to habit development success.
- Challenging forces that are barriers to habit development.

Tip the scale and make the empowering forces stronger than the challenging forces.
- Fulfill your role in the habit development process.
- Do not allow compromise or shortcuts.

- Leverage the accountability partner teams and make sure they take their roles seriously.
- Communicate the importance of the habit development plan at every opportunity.

In the first few weeks, the habit development planning team should meet to review progress weekly.
- Bring feedback to the meeting from other team members.
- Review measurement results and determine whether the team is on track and, if not, identify reasons for any gaps.
- Consider adjusting the plan, if necessary, based on gaps.

Consistent habit action execution is the focus.
- Do not allow exceptions.

Use your contingency plan when disruptions arise.
- Develop additional contingency plans, if necessary.

Real success is realized when a habit becomes so engrained that it becomes part of the team identity.

Make sure your new team members are fully trained in all the habits your team has developed.
- If this is not done, you run the real risk of losing momentum and suffering a setback.

If starting a new business, think carefully through the most important habits your new team members should practice.
- Before opening for business, make sure your team is trained in these habits to the point that they are part of the team identity.
- You can quickly build your business reputation on the success of these habits.

Monitor habit performance over time.
- If you determine that the habit is not being performed as consistently as originally planned, work with the team to develop a plan to improve performance.

Make continuous improvement a way of life for your team.
- Follow each successful habit development with another one.

IF YOU ENJOYED THIS BOOK, WOULD YOU DO ME A FAVOR?

Thank you for purchasing this book! It is an opportunity for me to help people learn how to apply habit theory to their lives so they may be more successful. I sincerely hope it is helpful to you.

Over the years, I've purchased hundreds of books from Amazon. In almost every case I first read reviews and they influenced my buying decision.

I did my very best to describe this book accurately. I hope you feel you are getting your money's worth. If you do, I would very much appreciate it if you would leave a review on Amazon.

This is very easy to do. Simply look the book up on Amazon, scroll down to Customer Reviews, and click on the box labeled "Write a customer review" just to the right of the graph showing the number and percent of reviews.

It will take you less than ten minutes to write a paragraph or two about your impression of the book.

Your review will be greatly appreciated by me and many potential buyers who use reviews to make a purchase decision.

If you are disappointed, please write to my personal email and give me an opportunity to make things right at Kyle@WorkTeamHabits.org

DO YOU HAVE QUESTIONS OR NEED ASSISTANCE?

I am happy to answer any questions you may have about building team habits. Please reach out to me at Kyle@WorkTeamHabits.org

Also, feel free to contact me at the same email address if you need assistance with your work team habit development program.

Finally, please remember that there are tools available on the website: Kyle@WorkTeamHabits.org

LIST OF POTENTIAL TEAM AND INDIVIDUAL REWARDS •⋯

AS PREVIOUSLY DISCUSSED, rewards may be team based or individual based. They may be intrinsic or extrinsic.   This section addresses potential extrinsic rewards.

Remember that you don't have to provide a reward to every team member. It is a good idea to do so with small rewards, but it may not be financially feasible with larger, more expensive rewards.   The solution to this is to set up either a draw or a point system.

DRAWS

In a reward draw, team members earn entries based on habit measurements.   There is no limit as to how many entries may be included in the draw, so this opens up a lot of possibilities to use it as an incentive for both team members and larger groups.   You may provide a draw for everyone on the team who works a shift in which the habit was performed after every cue. Accountability partners may earn entries in the draw if the accountability group of two or three consistently performs the habit. Individual team members may also earn entries.

Make sure all team members are clear on how entries are earned. This is best written down and posted then carefully followed by management or whoever is designated to provide entries when earned.

The draw should be held in front of several members of the team to make sure it looks, feels, and is fair. This can be done with a bit of showmanship so it is a motivating ritual.

POINT SYSTEM

Another method is to develop a point system.   Prizes are awarded based on points earned with more valuable prizes costing more points.

A fun alternative to the point system that allows you to limit the number of prizes you award is to provide play money instead of points as team members achieve certain measurement goals. Then, after several weeks or a few months, have a team meeting and "auction off" the rewards.   These types of events can be fun and provide management and the habit development planning team an opportunity to praise the team for developing the new habit and remind them how much it will impact the customer experience.

To get you started thinking of appropriate and valued rewards for your team, here is a list organized by several categories of reward types:

AWARDS
- Plaques
- Trophies
- Certificates

CARDS

- Thank you cards from leader
- Thank you cards from senior management

EXPERIENCES

- Hotel stay
- Theme park tickets
- Airplane tickets
- Helicopter ride
- Snowmobiling rental
- Segway rental
- Local tour
- Concert tickets
- Theater tickets
- Museum tickets
- Science Center tickets
- Team event at local park or beach
- Movie that the team watches at work
- Team bowling event
- Team putt putt golf event
- Team laser tag event
- Team paintball event
- Volunteer day in the local community
- Lunch with a senior executive
- Gym membership for a period of time
- Yoga class membership for a period of time
- Dance class membership for a period of time
- Upgrades on work travel
- Tour vendor of business
- Car of choice rented for a week
- Cooking class
- Subway pass
- Singing telegram
- King or queen for a day—with a crown and special privileges
- Family tours of the company with lunch
- Personal chef goes to their house and makes dinner for them and their family
- Sporting event tickets

- Confetti parade through the office

FOOD
- Team breakfast at a restaurant
- Team lunch at a restaurant
- Team dinner at a restaurant
- Donuts
- Bagels
- Pizza
- Cake
- Ice cream social
- Big decorated cookie
- Candy
- Bottle of wine (to consume at home)
- Picnic basket with food they can enjoy with their family

GENERAL
- Company stock
- Savings bond
- One month mortgage or rent payment

GIFT CARDS
- Movie ticket gift card/certificate
- Restaurant gift card
- Retail store gift card
- Putt-putt golf gift card
- Bowling gift card
- iTunes gift card
- Grocery store gift card
- Spa gift certificate
- Haircut/beauty salon gift certificate
- Amazon gift card

MERCHANDISE
- Pens with company logo
- Different pins that recognize different accomplishments
- Coffee cup with company logo
- Shirt with company logo or team name

- Backpack with company logo
- Balloons with company logo
- Computer bag with company logo
- Flowers
- Fruit basket
- Coffee gift basket
- Company themed gift basket
- Cookie gift basket
- Candy gift basket
- Engraved clocks
- Engraved paperweights
- Poster with inspiring quote
- Paperweight with inspiring quote
- Magazine subscription
- Digital book of choice
- Play money followed by an auction
- Car wash by the team leader
- "Let's Make A Deal" type of event where people pick from three boxes/closed offices, etc.
- Lottery ticket
- New office chair
- Video game of choice
- Smartphone for a year
- iPad
- Video game system
- New TV
- Silver dollar
- New personal computer
- Small plush animals
- Picture frames

PHOTO
- Team photographs
- Individual photograph

RECOGNITION
- Post photo of team in team member newsletter
- Post photo of team on team member website

- Post photo of team on bulletin board
- Post photo of team so it is visible to customers
- Create a press release and circulate it internally
- Wall of Achievement
- Parking space
- Standing ovation from the rest of the team
- Page in *Company Improvement History Book* documenting habit success
- Stickers to put in office (like merit badges)
- Corner office—reserve a corner office that the team member gets to work in for a month
- Name a conference room or break room after someone or a team. This might last a specific period of time
- Have an awards celebration (like the Academy Awards or Grammys)
- Name a special or item after them (e.g., "Cajun Chad's Chocolate Chip Pancakes")
- Decorations—balloons, streamers, etc.—for office
- Allow the team member to pick a charity for a company donation
- Notation on their record card
- Use the team member in a training video
- Notation on name tags

SPECIAL TREAT
- Home cleaning
- Yard work done
- Hire a baby sitter for the evening
- Free dry cleaning

TIME
- Extra break
- Extra day off
- Pick your schedule
- Free pass allowing the team member to arrive to work late
- Work from home
- One hour pass to leave work and run an errand
- Get their car washed and waxed

.

www.ingramcontent.com/pod-product-compliance
Lightning Source LLC
Chambersburg PA
CBHW051459170526
45166CB00001B/303